Becky Lynch

Book

THE MAN, THE MYTH, THE CHAMPION

Troy E Smithson

TABLE OF CONTENTS

PREFACE

When I was five years old, my dad told me, "Keep a journal." I wish I did. Back in the day, a quarter pound of sweets cost five pence; now it costs fifty. It would be interesting to track that."

I'm sure there were more intriguing topics I could have kept track of than the price of sweets, but that's where my lifelong passion for writing began. I've been journaling my entire life in the hopes that when I start writing my memoir, I'll be able to draw from a wealth of facts and experiences. However, things did not go quite as planned. While researching this book, I noticed that my writings resembled the repetitious ranting of a madwoman. Maybe not a madwoman, but certainly a lost girl trying to find her way in this crazy world, plagued by failed relationships, adolescent angst, and recurring difficulties.

Despite my diligent efforts to document how I was feeling at all times (and the cost of sweets, of course), I jotted down a few actual stories or experiences. However, my notebooks make it quite evident how much wrestling transformed my life permanently. It got into my circulation early on, and I don't think it could be removed even if I received a full transfusion.

You probably recognize me as Becky Lynch. If not, perhaps I served you at a pub in New York City or handed you peanuts high above the Atlantic. Perhaps you saw me murder a man with a shield on The Vikings or achieve octaves reserved only for Cyndi Lauper when I played her on NBC's Young Rock. Regardless, my professional life has been chaotic, and I intend to relive the most intriguing moments for you here. At times, I wish Rebecca Quin resembled the character I play on TV. Instead, she is vulnerable, often dumb, and far more complex. But I enjoy that about her.

CHAPTER 1

THE ENTRANCE

On January 30, 1987, in Limerick, Ireland, I made a prompt and stunning debut into the world.

My mother, who had just relocated her life to accommodate my father's new work, found out in the middle of labor that he had lost it. As she pushed me out of the dingy Limerick hospital, the radiator repairman abruptly interrupted to finish his final duty of the day.

"I beg your forgiveness, ma'am. Just a touch crowded here. I hope you have not been too cold. That is all fixed now. Goodbye, and congratulations, by the way. What a lovely little girl you have there."

Mom loaded up and moved back to Dublin City shortly after the radiator repairman wished us well.

Growing up, I thought my mother was the most gorgeous woman I'd ever seen. I know almost everyone says that about their mother, but I had validation. External validation. Professional validation. She was a model.

In fact, when the term "milf" was first coined, it appeared that the entire popular culture had been created particularly to mock my older brother, Richy, and myself.

When modeling became less steady, she swapped in her calendar centerfold job for the equally glamorous (at the time) life of a globe-trotting flight attendant.

Her stunning beauty gave me hope that one day, when the puberty fairies bestowed their favors on me, I would be able to gain this arcane talent. However, these fairies appear to have overlooked the "make her a stunner" component of their growth dust.

Or, rather, my invention of the potato waffle and cheese white bread sandwich enslaved my taste buds at the age of nine, trapping me in their starchy, creamy cage while keeping those cellulite mounds on my thighs fed and happy.

It wasn't only that I admired my mother because she was breathtakingly beautiful. She exuded humility, almost as if she were ignorant of the attention she received at every turn. She was a diligent worker as well as a firm believer in reality.

All of these characteristics combined to make her marriage to my father extremely bewildering.

Don't get me wrong; my father was an absolute legend. He was a dreamer, a charmer, a man with his head in the clouds who loved creativity and uniqueness above all else. He was continually devising the next breakthrough idea. But his ideas always appeared to outpace his execution. Dad never got his footing in life, yet dad was most proud of me and my brother.

My brother was an angel, but I was Satan with a badly cut bob. My father would admonish Richy for hitting his brother in the head with a frying pan, saying, "Just leave her alone!" "She is expressing herself."

My parents are probably the most diametrically different people I've ever encountered. My father respected freedom and autonomy. My mother's first words to me were, "Be normal." Even at age five, I knew I was going to shatter her heart. For the majority of his life, my father was both employed and unemployed. My mother always had steady employment. They could only agree on one thing: they loved me and my brother more than anything else, and we should always come first.

To me, their opposing personalities were a blessing. My father gave me the guts to dream. My mother gave me the practicality to go out and work for it. My mother gave me hope that I'd grow up to be a babe. My father diluted the gene pool sufficiently that I realized I needed to focus on my personality.

By the time I was a year old, they had decided to end their marriage and separate, which was extremely looked upon in Catholic Ireland, where divorce was not even allowed.

It did not have a significant impact on my life. (A) I was too little to understand what was going on, and (B) by the time I was four and old enough to notice my father wasn't present, my mother permitted Dad to return to our house in an act of really admirable parenting. In every way, this was a success.

We could have our father, and she had assistance when she needed to go away on longer vacations.

Sure, living with your ex seems like a nightmare, and they didn't chat or interact much, and there was always an undercurrent of tension in the house that we were too little to grasp. However, they were nice enough to do things as a family. Vacations, banquets, and gatherings—you name it.

For Richy and me, everything was OK while our parents continued their separate celibacy lives under one roof—a nostalgic assumption shared by all children.

It also meant we didn't have to spend time away from our typical lower-middle-class Dublin neighborhood, where every day was a kids' party. There were around seventeen of us young hooligans, all of similar ages, running around causing mayhem, with little drama breaking out between us.

Until we were invaded by the British during the summer of 1997. One of the neighbors invited their English grandson, Robbie, to stay while school was out. The boy has Dwayne "The Rock" Johnson's charm packed into his small, sixty-pound physique. He danced and sang for the enjoyment of everyone on the block. Everyone but me. I've never liked this man. I'm not sure what it was about him. Perhaps I was jealous of how popular he was among my peers. Maybe I envy his rhythm and his beautiful singing voice. Or, just maybe, this kid was a little jerk.

One day, while Robbie sat in a tree above me in the hood's shared green area, most likely singing "Bohemian Rhapsody," I swung from our homemade swing below. It was essentially a rope slung from a branch, with a little plank to sit on. Our many hours of dragging our feet in the same location had made a dent in the packed dirt beneath.

Suddenly, the rope snapped! I landed on my ass with a loud thump.

"She's so fat she broke the swing!" Robbie roared and laughed hysterically.

My pals and I all laughed together.

I sat there humiliated and tried not to cry.

When the need had passed and I had summoned all of my courage, I stood up and brushed myself off. Only to discover that I had landed directly on top of the indentation in the ground.

"She made a dent in the ground! Hahahahahaha!"

Everyone laughed again.

I couldn't stop crying this time, so I ran inside.

I grabbed the plank and ran home in tears. Then I was determined to lose weight so that I might be like my mother when I grew up. But then I was hungry, unhappy, and all I wanted was pizza. Beauty was my mother's realm. Pizza was mine.

CHAPTER 2

THE UNDERDOG

My mother was burnt out after only two years of dating Chris - her boyfriend. She was working full-time, flying across the world, cultivating a blooming romance, and raising a complete asshole of a teenager. (That'd be me).

She chose to search for houses closer to Chris in Bayside, Dublin, which is around thirty minutes from where we reside. She might as well have wanted to relocate to India, given how far away it appeared to my thirteen-year-old self. And, of course, this meant that everything would change!

I'd have to leave the home I grew up in. I'd need to change schools. I would have to leave all of my pals. My father would have to move out.

"Why can't Chris just move closer to where we live?" I bargained.

"Because his kids' mother lives closer to him and he has to see his kids too."

I did not enjoy any of this! I felt as if our family was getting shafted while he was being catered to.

In adulthood, my mother was looking for a way out of the tension-filled house that had in many ways kept her hostage in her own home—as one might assume while cohabiting with one's ex-husband. Plus, Chris was a fantastic man who had shown to be an incredible companion for my mother, and it was about time they moved past this stupid awkward situation. She also refused to move in with him, fearing that living with someone other than our father would be unpleasant for my brother and me. And I'm confident I'll spare Chris my youthful rage.

After months of searching, as if by miracle, the house next door to Chris became available for sale, and my mother immediately made her move.

It rained on a moving day, which exactly reflected my emotions. We will disregard the fact that it rains almost every day in Ireland.

As I left the only home I'd ever known, I yelled at my mother, "I hate you," with venom I don't think I've spat since.

My father tried to comfort me as he led me to the car, but I was too far gone. He despised her, too. He'd had a successful nearly ten-year run. He adored his children above everything else, and he was forced to leave them. He couldn't afford much in terms of housing, which automatically disqualified him for majority custody.

Mom's new house was a fixer-upper that bordered on decrepit. The previous proprietors definitely dabbled in street-level pharmaceutical sales, as evidenced by their triple-beam scale and a constellation of burn marks all over the carpet.

The stress I was causing my mother was taking its toll on her. She started losing away, unable to eat and gagging at the dinner table when she tried. She always wanted to be a good mother, have nice children, and live a happy life. However, no matter how many masses she attended, things were not going as planned for her. Unfortunately, my situation was only going to worsen over the next few years.

Furthermore, the new community was a maze of seedy side lanes and nettle-filled fields, complete with a weird ancient graveyard in the middle. Perfect for delinquent teenagers, of which there were plenty. This aided my newfound hobbies of street drinking and pot smoking, which I had taken up to cope with all of my thirteen-year-old emotions.

On the plus side, my brother and I were growing closer, bonding over our mutual dislike for our current circumstances. Richy was four years my senior, and while I had frustrated the living shit out of him for the majority of our lives, he had the patience of a saint, and all I wanted to be was like him. He is one of life's decent people, an old soul with an instinctive sense of wisdom.

Richy also excels at whatever he sets his mind to. While I never had many interests beyond hanging out with my friends and watching TV, he was always doing something productive—karate, guitar, rugby—but his true passion was creating art. He was gifted from an early age, creating comic book characters and removing asphalt from roadways on hot summer days to build his own action figures. And, while being older, smarter, and more accepting than I was, he was also battling with the deterioration of our family, possibly even more so, as he tried to manage his own pain while simultaneously serving as my shield of armor. When my parents were arguing, he bore the brunt of it so that I would be less affected.

Throughout these transitions, we found solace in two things.

Wrestling is number one. Of course, we were all Hulkamaniacs in the early 1990s, singing along to "Real American" as the balding, bandana-clad hero flaunted his twenty-four-inch pythons to the delight of all who watched. But once I passed the age of five, it was no longer fashionable to enjoy wrestling. After a long hiatus from all things WWE, my brother renewed his love for the sport, which meant I was bound to follow suit. It was the height of the Attitude Era, when wrestling was bold and brash, beating up your boss only resulted in more money, the objectification of women was strangely celebrated, characters were outlandish, and it had just become cool for teenagers and people in their twenties to re-indulge, while classrooms were filled with kids giving each other the middle finger and telling their teachers to "suck it."

But I wasn't going to take wrestling's coolness for granted. It would need to prove itself to me. Because I was definitely the authority on cool.

"That stuff is for babies," I mocked my brother while he watched. "Don't you know it's all fake?" I was the absolute worst.

"Actually, it has gotten really good," Richy said calmly, unconcerned by my comments.

And while I was doing my own thing around the house, listening to Nirvana or writing about my problems in journal entries, I kept one eye on the television—thanks to one mesmerizing artist.

His name was Mick Foley, and he was in a feud with Triple H. Mick, a huge and hairy man missing half an ear and with the physique of a springtime bear, had a unique style of communicating that captivated me. Something about the way this guy narrated a story, with his slightly high-pitched and cracked voice, drew me in. He was intense and warm in equal measure. He was brave but vulnerable, with wonderful comedic timing. More than anything, he was genuine. Through my television screen, I could see he was a nice person.

I could relate to Mick when I was a teenager and felt like I didn't fit in. He, like myself, was not born with extraordinary abilities. He wasn't athletic, but he compensated by taking massive risks in the ring, and I really wanted those risks to pay off for him.

I began telling my brother, "Just call me when Mick comes on!"

Mick would appear on television and entice me—and then I was hooked. One of my life objectives would be to give Mick Foley a big bear embrace someday. I don't want to reveal the book's ending.

(But, tick).

Wrestling is a weird sport. Once you're into it, you can't stop talking about it. Or at least, I couldn't. The spectacle, the plotlines, the conflict and resolve. The athletic moves, the stunts, good triumphing over evil, and even if things aren't going well for our heroes, victory is just around the corner. It included everything: drama, comedy, romance, adrenaline, and thrill. Above all, it contained hope.

I admired the hard work, training, devotion, and tenacity it takes to become a WWE superstar. Even though I knew nothing about discipline, I could live vicariously via my idols.

I wanted to discuss everything about wrestling with everyone. I wanted to break down the intricacy in the ring as well as the chatter outside of it. And I discovered a place I could go on indefinitely, which leads me to number two: the Central Bank. I'm sure you're thinking, What a strange thing for a thirteen-year-old to be into. I was more interested in the bank's location than in banking itself. It was in the heart of Dublin City and became a gathering place for misfits of all kinds. The goths, hippies, rockers, and emos would all go there on weekends to drink away our common unhappiness, connecting over our dysfunctional families and love of alternative music, as well as wrestling.

Back in my new neighborhood, I had acquired a group of friends. We all shared a love of getting stoned and hanging out on the mean streets of Bayside. Everyone was slightly older than me, which made buying booze even easier.

With my mother gone overnight on weekends, our house became the party house. Most weekends were rather quiet, but every now and again, the wrong individual would invite the wrong bunch of people. Then my brother and I had to keep fights from breaking out and individuals from setting fire to our furniture.

My mother could smell smoke when she went into the home, jet-lagged and weary from working all night. She'd begin feverishly cleaning, disappointed in us and exhausted by our negligence and recklessness.

Of course, we would vehemently reject everything. Innocent until proven guilty! And she had no tangible evidence that swarms of delinquent adolescents were using her home as if it were a local nightclub.

My aunt, observing my wildness—and perhaps assuming she could extinguish the fires, given she was a former wild woman herself—took me to Italy with her and her family for two weeks during the summer, in the hopes of providing me with some grounding and life experiences.

The first week was packed with tourism and historical trips. Traveling through Pompeii, visualizing the world two thousand years ago and the horror people suffered as their town was smothered in molten lava, reminded me of the insignificance of my concerns and that things might not be as bad as they seemed. Especially when I spent my evenings eating authentic Italian pizza and the world's best gelato.

However, when it was time to relax and lounge by the pool, I was less than enthusiastic. My chubby fourteen-year-old frame and frizzed-up mop of hair made me feel self-conscious, so I did everything I could to avoid wearing a bikini in public.

One day, while I sat next to my aunt, attempting awkwardly to conceal my body, she did her best to console me. "Oh, Becky darling," she responded with a smile, "there's far too many blond beauties around here for anyone to be looking at you."

Oh, gee. Thank you. That makes me freaking happy.

She quickly realized that I was just as difficult as my mother said. I pouted all day, covertly smoked my cigarettes, and stockpiled wine in my room, refusing to interact with anyone. But Italy is truly beautiful in the summer.

When school resumed, I had completely withdrawn within myself, with little interest in anything beyond getting high in the bushes at lunch break. I even failed PE, which I assumed you had passed simply by turning up. And I was there with bloodshot eyes, reluctant to do anything. I was worried about how dumb I looked when I ran. To be fair, as high as I was, my concern was likely justified.

My mother left the school in tears after being waterboarded with stories about how lethargic and uninterested I was, how I was falling behind, and what needed to be done.

I knew I wasn't doing well, and I had no qualms about making my mother cry on my behalf, but when someone else did it, it was different. It felt as if there was a remote possibility that I was the source of the problem and needed to take action.

As I sat in my depressing bedroom, debating the meaning of things and if school was important or if a better way to deal with this confusion was to find a can of beer and relax in the graveyard beside the house, I had an epiphany. I needed to change my life for good right now.

But how?

I entered the computer room and found Richy gazing at a black-and-maroon webpage.

"What's NWA Hammerlock?" I inquired, reading the text at the top of the screen. It sounded like either a rap band or a particularly aggressive shark. Perhaps both.

"It's a wrestling school in the UK."

"Oh, cool!" I commented, wondering whether he was reconsidering his art career.

Earlier that week, we had watched WWE's new show Tough Enough, in which individuals with no prior wrestling experience learnt the craft from scratch. The training was horrible, and the bumps appeared terrible. However, most people remained with it because the promotion featured two winners—one male and one female.

It was hard to watch since these aspiring stars would frequently drop out of fitness tests or moan about being sore or injured. "Stop being a little bitch!" I would yell at the TV. "This is your dream, everyone!!! You're extremely lucky! How could you demonstrate any weakness?! It's WWE, for goodness sake!"

Richy and I both knew we could perform better (my athletic inadequacies were a minor detail), so I assumed he was studying up NWA Hammerlock.

"I wrote to them and said I wanted to train. I said I'm not a dreamer, and I know how much work it will take, but I feel like I'd regret not trying," Richy explained as he went through the website and landed on the talent list.

He was a full-grown adult at nineteen, but my mother would never allow my fifteen-year-old self to fly to England to train as a wrassler.

A few days later, Andre Baker, the proprietor of Hammerlock, wrote back to accept Richy's application. In a lovely turn of events, he revealed that Paul Tracy and that douchey-looking Fergal Devitt would be starting a wrestling school in Ireland in May.

My brother, like my mother, was not going to support my newfound wrestling goals right away. In fact, if she ever entered the room when we were wrestling, she would scream, avoid her gaze, and flee as if she had caught us watching some terrible pornography. As a result, she wouldn't have had a chance to object when I told her I was going to do Brazilian jiu-jitsu, which sounded far more exotic.

Fortunately for me, my father was always willing to back whatever eccentric whim I had.

Training started at 2:00 p.m. on Sunday, so I spent the night before with my father.

"This looks like the spot," my father declared as we arrived twenty minutes early at the school, which was actually simply the gymnasium of a nearby primary school. Needless to say, there was no huge metal "NWA Ireland" sign above the door.

"Don't come in!" I told my father as I stepped out of the car. Nothing would have been more uncool or a dead giveaway of my youth than my father accompanying me on my first day.

"As you wish, missy."

I hopped out of the car and dashed across the grounds, hoping to avoid getting drenched on this typically rainy Sunday. I wore my hoodie over my head to keep my freshly colored red hair from flowing down my shirt, and I pulled up my baggy slacks to keep the bottoms from being soaked in grass.

I walked up anxiously, pushed open the double doors, and turned left into the corridor. It was time for my ultimate plan. If I say I'm sixteen, they'll be on me. They might even ask for ID, which would be embarrassing. I'll tell them I'm seventeen, and they won't suspect anything!

"Hello," a sing-songy voice said to me. Fergal Devitt's profile photo did not do him justice. He was stunning, personable, confident, and one of those kinds you couldn't help but be pulled to; there was a sense that he would go on to achieve huge things one day—which he has, as Finn Balor in WWE—and, most importantly, he was not at all douchey. He sat at a table, with a sign-up sheet in front of him: name, age, phone number, and money.

"Rebecca Quin, 17, January 30th, 1985, 0868918980," a beautifully folded ten-euro bill courtesy of my father.

"Go ahead," Fergal responded without asking for ID as he led me into the hall, demonstrating my master plan was successful!! I am a damned genius!

I looked around the room, which was well lit. It was nothing like what I had expected. There were no behemoths looming over me. There were around twelve teenage lads, some tall and gangly, others short and slender, and some with their hair halfway grown out in that uncomfortable period. Some were a little chubby, and one or two appeared to have lifted some weights but also enjoyed a burger and a beer. I did a double take. I was also the lone girl in my class. It seemed oddly reassuring. I had gone from being the least fit girl in my PE class to becoming the most fit female in my wrestling class. Even in the worst-case scenario, no matter how horrible I am at this, I am still the best girl here.

Most shockingly, there was no illuminated wrestling ring with bright red ropes and a black canvas. Actually, there was no wrestling ring at all! There were only six blue padded mats on the floor.

When everyone came, Paul and Fergal greeted the class.

"We don't yet have a wrestling ring, but it should arrive within the next two weeks. Meanwhile, we'll get you started with the essentials."

"Basics" was correct. We started with a quick and simple warm-up that included a few air squats and jumping jacks, nothing like the fitness tests I'd seen on Tough Enough. I came here prepared to puke, for crying out loud!

Next up, bumping. I'd seen folks struggling with this on television. I was not going to be one of those folks. I was not going to be a wimp about it. Simply fall backwards, tuck your chin, land on the upper portion of your back, and hit the mat. Simple as that. How difficult could it be?

My brother, who had now created as much space between us as possible, offered to go first.

His first bump was flawless, as if he had practiced it since birth. Just got out of the womb and landed a nice flat back. Asshole.

Next in line was Kenny, a tiny, slender boy who resembled Frankie Muniz and weighed no more than 100 pounds. He also landed perfectly.

I knew this trash would be a piece of piss, I reasoned, their expertise instilling confidence in me.

They were followed by a tall, gangly boy.

That was a long way to fall, I thought.

He certainly agreed.

He slumped clumsily to the ground as he attempted to defend himself. I started coaching him in my brain, like the armchair guru I'd become: just commit! Land on your back; what are you doing, sissy-boy?

He couldn't hear my telepathic instructions, so he kept landing on his elbows or trying to break his fall in the most painful way imaginable. What a shame, I thought.

"Who's next?"

That was my cue to leap in. Something I've learned from failing at most things is to take your turn when the bar appears to be at an all-time low. That way, there's only one way up!

"I'll go!" I volunteered eagerly.

I stood on the blue mat. Arms crossed over my chest, ready to throw myself backwards and—for the first time in my life—be a complete natural at something.

Thud, thud, thud. I fell unimpressively—not smoothly on the upper portion of my back, but on my lower back, then my elbows, upper back, and head. My hands did not slap the mat as I expected. More like giving it a wimpy high five, Napoleon Dynamite style. Also, Ouch! That freaking hurt.

Fergal instructed, "Not quite... kick your legs out and try slapping the mat."

That's what I was aiming to do!!

"Yeah, of course," I murmured.

I tried again. This time, only three thuds. Back, elbows, and the back of my head. The smack was likewise waiflike.

"Give it a go again."

Thump, thud. Ooooof. This time, I had winded myself. The mats didn't provide much padding, given that there was concrete just an inch underneath.

When the lesson ended, we had learned how to bump, lock up, exchange a few holds, and even do a small exhibition match at the end.

As bad as I was, to my relief—or so I persuaded myself—I wasn't the worst person there. Poor, lanky fucker.

My body ached when I woke up the next day. My neck ached from the repetitive whiplash, but I couldn't wait to catch the bus to school and tell my pals all about it.

I had discovered something I loved. I wasn't very good at it, but I wanted to be, so that felt more important.

But now I needed to look the part. Become jacked, stacked, ripped, lean, and mean. Gainzzzzzzzzzzz, baby! Except I had no idea about nutrition. I only knew that jacked individuals drank protein drinks. So, I purchased my first tub of protein powder. Bye-bye, flabville; here I come, muscletown.

I eagerly opened the white tub and gagged at the fumes that followed. It smelt like a two-thousand-pound man who lived on eggs and stale cheese had imprisoned his farts in the powder I was going to eat. I pinched my nose and choked back the thick, gloopy fluid, anxiously trying not to puke. There must be a better solution.

I wanted shoulders and abs like my hero Lita, the sassy female spitfire I'd seen doing backflips on TV, but maybe not so badly yet.

I concluded that my best shot was to quit drinking and smoking and follow the fad of the time: a low-fat diet consisting primarily of bread, spaghetti, rice, and more bread. I planned to make a body from the gods, loaf by loaf.

CHAPTER 3

THE HAMMERLOCK

We arrived at Sittingbourne, Kent, following a two-hour train ride from the airport. Richy took out the directions he had scrawled on a piece of paper and led us down a creepy-looking alley until we reached an equally creepy-looking side door. There in front of us stood a wrestling ring that had clearly seen better days. Like in 1972, when it was likely new. We were in the right place.

To the right of the ring, there was a bar with three or four small dark wooden tables. The place was full of dodgy-looking old men. The proprietor, Andre Baker, was the most suspicious of them all, as if he had stepped out of a Guy Ritchie film and into this run-down gym. He was bald, short, and broad, covered in hideous tattoos, and had eyes that bulge out of his skull like a pug. Despite his frightening appearance, Andre exuded warmth and charisma. He was a shady geezer, but a lovely one at that. The bar was solely for wrestlers. I can't think Andre had a liquor license. But it allowed him to make some extra money while also allowing all of the wrestlers to decompress after a long day of practice, and no one was going to snitch because Andre was an intimidating young man.

Hammerlock has appeared on a television show called Faking It. The idea was that people from many walks of life would train under a certain discipline for four weeks. At the end of the program, they'd demonstrate their newly acquired talents alongside three actual professionals in their chosen field.

To my fifteen-year-old self, everybody who appeared on it looked like an A-list celebrity.

As other roster members came in during the day, we would nudge each other as if John Cena himself had entered the room. One was a tall, blond, and breathtakingly gorgeous twenty-one-year-old man who was completely insane. I saw him on Faking It and instantly fell in love. Or I thought he was attractive—same difference at fifteen. It turned out that he liked me, too. That was the only alternative, as I was once again the sole girl in the camp.

Following our first day of training, I spent the evening in the filthy side alley, flirting with the British stud. And, after a few drinks at the bar and no reservations, we were making out in the middle of a roundabout up the road. I adored this camp! Not only was I able to pursue and better my passion, but for the first time in my life, gorgeous men were paying attention to me, and I didn't even have to stalk them!

The days were long—nine hours of wrestling in a hot gym in the midst of the summer without air conditioning. You could sleep on the mats, in the ring, under the ring, or, if you were really lucky, on the crash pad. After partying till three or four in the morning, we were woken up at 8:00 a.m. by Chester, a pit bull with the largest pair of testicles I'd ever seen on a mammal. Chester would come in bouncing across our motionless heads, teabagging anyone who happened to have an open mouth.

The bright lights were then turned on, and it was back to the bar for another round. Only this time, it's in small plastic cups filled with awful instant coffee. Then check the mirror to see if someone had shaved your brows in the middle of the night. Ribbing was alive and thriving in the NWA UK wrestling tradition.

Over the course of a week, the class came together to tie one lad up in red duct tape and hang him upside down like a gigantic fish as we posed for photos. I saw one person shave his pubic hair and push it into another's open mouth while he slept. The owner of a huge bottle of cider left it unattended for a pee break, only to return and, after a large, pleasurable drink, discover that someone had taken a pee break in his cider bottle.

Fortunately, my brother and I went home uninjured, but exhausted. A full week of such routine, along with nothing more food than KFC French fries and Dooley's toffee liqueur, had not done our bodies any favors. However, my wrestling had improved considerably.

I returned to school a few weeks later, full of the thrill of a summer of wrestling, as well as the newfound confidence that comes from committing to a talent.

Even more exciting, Paul and Fergal stated that we would be hosting our very first wrestling show! In front of an actual crowd. After wrestling for just over six months, my first performance was scheduled for November 11, 2002. My training was about to get really intense. My diet of bread and water would be sufficient—no deviating off track now, Becky; the time has come!

As someone who had never really done anything in life, save maybe chasing boys, I found it rewarding to discover that hard work did pay dividends.

The week before the show, Paul and Fergal assembled the class to reveal the card. We stood around the ring, waiting for our names to be called. When they got to the big event, my name had not been called.

I didn't get a match, so my consolation was to work as a valet for my brother, who now went by the great name Gonzo de Mondo. I did not want to be a valet. I wanted to be a wrestler. I'm sure my brother didn't want to babysit me during his debut match, either.

However, I was sent to the commission battle royal. That is where they put the individuals that sucked. Along with practically everyone else—who'd previously played matches—in an attempt to fill out the numbers.

I was crushed.

I tried to persuade myself that it was only because I was the only girl. It could convey a poor message if a male beats up a girl. But Chyna has to do it, dang it! And with a few more years of my brioche-based diet, I'd have muscles like hers!

The day of the concert, the audience of family and friends buzzed outside the curtain as we all prepared to go out and wow them with the best wrestling they had ever witnessed. I looked around at the group of young men in tight booty shorts, greasing themselves up with baby oil and making jokes as if they had done this before. Wasn't everyone else terrified of what was beyond that curtain? Social rejection? Public humiliation?

As I wondered how I would fare. Should I Have My Own Singles Match? One day, my brother was getting ready to make his entry, as relaxed as if he were about to order a McDonald's Happy Meal. I, on the other hand, could feel my lunch reappearing in the bottom of my throat.

Finally, it was time for my moment. I executed my maneuver reasonably well. To describe it another way would be a falsehood. Please, the audience went crazy! It was enough for Gonzo to use his finisher, the Demondo Driver! One, two, and three!! It's all done!! So this is what winning is like.

But I still had to go to the battle royal! Normally, in a battle royal, the winner is determined after all other opponents have been hurled over the top rope, leaving one person standing alone in the ring, victorious.

The difficulty with the battle royal in this case, apart from the fact that it was primarily made up of the class's rejects, was that we hadn't yet learned to climb the top rope. Given that inexperience, the stipulation became that if you landed on your back, you were out of the match. It rapidly became difficult for the audience to grasp since the ring was filled with uncomfortable people huddled together. Several times, people slipped or botched their own maneuvers, landing on their backs and hopping up, hoping no one noticed. Everyone noticed. And nobody was impressed.

I took a body slam from a larger gentleman and rolled out abruptly, relieved.

Aside from the battle royale, I was on a high. The exhilaration of performing, the fact that there were over 200 people in the audience and they shouted for me. Becky's belly is like a sack of potatoes.

Wrestling was now in my veins, and it was not going away.

I was now a pro wrestler. Sure, I hadn't made any money, but I was a performer and couldn't wait for the next show.

CHAPTER 4

HART ATTACK

Every February, Hammerlock performed tours across the United Kingdom. They were considered a big thing because not only did you get to wrestle every night for a week, but these tours also included a large name, generally someone who had previously wrestled for WWE. On this particular trip, Andre had booked Jim "The Anvil" Neidhart, a former WWE tag-team champion and half of the Hart Foundation. One of WWE's best tag pairings.

These visits provided nothing but invaluable knowledge, but Andre believed it would be a good idea to hold a match to showcase the new affiliate, NWA Ireland.

Paul and Fergal were tasked with handpicking two guys who constantly put up the best matches, and, of course, my natural brother was chosen, as was another trainee named Carl.

I asked my brother, "Can I come?"

"No," he said without hesitation.

I simply wanted to study and develop. To immerse oneself in the wrestling world and seize any opportunities that arise. Even if such chances were not necessarily presented to me. Really, I was like Robin Hood. Taking from the opportunity rich (Richy) and giving to the opportunity poor (me). I tagged along like a bothersome ailment.

I even managed to get onto the card and valeted for Fergal and Paul. Of course, this time I took no offense at becoming a valet, knowing I was already pushing my luck by being there. Plus, who knows when a better chance will arise.

It turns out it wouldn't take long. On the final day of the tour, I was booked in a six-person tag team match! I was supposed to pair up with Fergal and Paul to face off against Danny Williams, Ciara Wilde, and Jim "The Anvil" Neidhart!!!

At sixteen years old and with eight months of wrestling experience, I was about to face a WWE superstar. The only difficulty was that I didn't know what I was doing.

At the start of the contest, all three of us attacked Jim. In my haste, I kicked him straight in the kneecap, causing his massive hamstring to twist in the incorrect direction. Out of legitimate dread of losing an ACL, he shoved me hard, scolding me in his thick American accent, "You don't kick people like that!" with a voice that erupted from the pit of his diaphragm.

All of my enthusiasm changed to embarrassment as I slunk back and rested by the ropes, hoping I didn't mess anything else up or damage anyone. My first genuine opportunity, and I nearly kneecapped the star of the performance.

The match ended, and I hurried sadly to the back, waiting for Jim to return so I could profusely repent for nearly putting him in the hospital.

Thankfully, he had calmed down over the brief walk from ring to curtain. As he passed through, a big lump of red flesh coated in perspiration and hair, I approached cautiously.

"Sir, I apologize. "I didn't mean to hurt you."

"Oh, honey," he murmured with his sweetest dad voice. "That is okay. Let me show you how to hit people."

He moved me to the side, out of sight of everyone.

"You see the leg doesn't bend that way, so you're better off hitting here—like this."

Despite his massive stature, he delivered a club to the back that felt like I had been hit by a marshmallow.

My worry of him blacklisting me has subsided. Thank goodness, since this week had been so much fun, and I couldn't wait to do it again.

It was a turf battle. A battle for domination. Like Springfield vs. Shelbyville in The Simpsons. We were the first school and promotion in the neighborhood. Someone else coming in and attempting to steal our market was outright treason.

We were NWA Ireland. The first one. The first.

They were doing Irish Whip Wrestling (IWW). The impostors. The fraudsters. The promotion for Dublin babes who lacked the courage to take the train to Bray to learn how to become true professional wrestlers. And I despised them. I despised what they stood for. I despised their silly moniker and everyone who wrestled for them.

Even worse, I despised the fact that they were putting on their first show in my school hall! In most places of the world, this is considered treason. They could as well have come up to my house, opened the windows and doors, and had each of their "wrestlers" piss on the furnishings.

Furthermore, these fraudsters had the arrogance to bring American and Canadian wrestlers over to promote their show as if it were a greater issue than it actually was. (You left Jim Neidhart out of this!)

Of course, the impression in Ireland that anyone from America was somewhat of a big deal was still alive and well in the early 2000s, following Bill Clinton's auld triumph, when fascination with all things USA was at an all-time high. Canada, of course, received the brunt of the criticism, because who could tell the difference?

In an act of pure hatred, disguised as support, a group of Springfield residents went to the event to check on our competitors, ready to mock at their poor attempts to court a crowd or put on an appropriate wristlock.

We arrived early to ensure we got fantastic seats and could hear us yell our overly passionate chants, which messed with their heads. Were we genuine? Was this a mockery? Nobody could blame us for certain. But let there be no doubt about it. It was an infiltration.

The show began. The sleazy ring announcer appeared like an evil circus boss, ready to proclaim his stars for the night.

Unfortunately for us, these fuckers did had potential.

The first match of the night featured a man named Joe Cabray, who possessed biceps like Hulk Hogan's 24-inch pythons. What was this youngster doing in a promotion like that? Didn't he want to practice with real wrestlers? The best wrestlers? The toughest wrestlers?

Yes, several of our boys had some muscles. But some of their lads were mostly muscles, with heads protruding from their huge necks.

Sheamus O'Shaunessy was a six-three-year-old muscle-bound freak with hair as orange as a tangerine and skin so pale he was virtually transparent.

We mocked its true Irishness. He seemed to be trying to catch Vince McMahon's attention from this school hall, which had two hundred people in attendance.

"Pffft. As if. "I bet he can't work for shit," we muttered, thinking we were the authority on labor.

We instantly shut up as we witnessed him beat the living snot out of some poor young man. Knowing full well that if Sheamus sticks to it, he will be picked up by WWE in a hurry. What a sellout.

I also got to look at my direct competitors. Much like I was the lone female in NWA Ireland, they had their token lady, a short, hefty woman named Alex Breslin. I loathed her. It was primitive. She had the audacity to compete in my hometown. I was the lone female wrestler in Ireland. This was my land. My kingdom. Who did she believe she was? I was going to take her down in the only way I knew how. With phony kindness.

I cheered for her with all in my body, not wanting anyone to know how jealous I was.

I told myself, "She'll never make it. She lacks toughness."

This island was not large enough for both of us. Only one of us was able to make it. And it definitely wasn't going to be her.

Their main event pitted their trainer Blake Norton, a "Canadian" Simon had brought in to try to derail our promotion (or so we thought), against another Canadian superstar named Scotty Mac. A jacked and tanned pretty lad with more real-life charisma than anyone I'd ever seen before. Blake Norton, it turned out, was not actually from Canada. He'd recently spent six weeks training in Calgary and returned with a Canadian accent. He was swiftly exposed for not having as much experience as he claimed when IWW began to host shows and established wrestlers discovered how awful he was.

When the show ended, we stayed to present ourselves as competitors. Scotty even invited me to the after-party that night, indicating that our phony niceness had been misinterpreted as genuine.

Sure, I'll cavort with the enemy. Allow this stupid Canadian to see the folly of his ways. He is simply a talent for rent. He is unaware that he could have wrestled for Ireland's biggest wrestling company. If we had the money to pay him. Or anyone, really. But it didn't matter. It was the principle!

CHAPTER 5

THE DECISION

If I was going to drop out of college to pursue my wrestling career, the ideal time would be when my mother was halfway across the world and couldn't yell at me.

Fortunately for me, that opportunity occurred in January 2005, when Mom and Chris traveled to Australia to visit my stepbrother.

To reassure her, I informed her that I would change college courses, possibly to something more sports-related, given that I had miraculously become some sort of athlete in the last two years. But while I'm waiting, I might as well gain some life experience, build some villages, and see if there's any chance for me outside the confines of my small island.

But, where? America or Canada? Both featured opulent wrestling scenes, and America boasted the largest promotions in the world.

Wrestling in Japan became my ultimate aim. In contrast to American wrestling, where women have a long history of being considered as sideshows or sex objects, Japanese companies portrayed their ladies as talented performers and combatants. I just had one Japanese women's wrestling VHS video, but it was my most prized possession: a golden chalice of plastic and metal with the outline of my future. The women outperformed any man I'd seen. They were high fliers that hit hard and swiftly. I had no idea if I'd ever be able to match their powers, but I was determined to try. However, I had no idea where to start. Plus, I didn't know the language. So it got me back to my original two choices.

Obtaining a visa for America was more difficult, and coming over there on my own and not knowing anyone, having just turned eighteen, seemed a little scarier, what with all the guns and such.

I didn't know anyone in Canada either, but I had met Scotty Mac at the IWW show a year before, when he spent most of the evening bragging about the richness and popularity of promotions in British Columbia.

And if things really got bad, I had a cousin who resided on Vancouver Island. Yes, I had only met him once when I was twelve, but family is family.

Vancouver was a go. With this solid basis of two people I hardly knew.

I was resolved to create something of myself.

If I didn't succeed by the end of the year, I'd return and attend college, like I promised my mother.

With time running out before embarking on the journey of a lifetime, I began saying my goodbyes to all of my friends and family who had given me eighteen years of memories. I believed that the more final I made this, and the more pressure I put on myself, the more likely I was to succeed.

There were only three days left when I saw Fergal in town to say farewell. After all, I would not have experienced this dream if he hadn't opened the school in Bray. We had been growing closer and closer since the UK tour, when we nearly became accomplices to a crime. We'd chat about wrestling and our goals, knowing that staying in Ireland wouldn't get us anywhere. We had to take chances, travel, step out on a limb, and put ourselves out there.

And I think by laughing and flirting all day throughout town, we were putting ourselves out there. Just in a different manner. After four hours of excitement and anticipation, it was that horrible time of day when we had to return to our different homes in opposite directions. As we stood at the train station, I looked to the electric board above, which warned me that I had four minutes to make a move or be doomed to travel to the Pacific Northwest with a suitcase full of what-ifs. I went for it right there, kissing him in the middle of Dublin's busiest station, my knees almost buckling with glee.

But now that love was on my mind, the last thing I wanted to do was leave!

The time that was supposed to be spent packing and preparing was quickly replaced with going on hikes and lying on the beach, gazing into each other's eyes and enjoying those lovely vulnerable moments that leave a lingering sense of magic in the air like youthful love. The yearning to leave and the desire to stay drew me in opposite directions, as if I were about to split in two. At the same time, it seemed like everything I could possibly want in life was occurring.

I now had a guy who I had previously considered was much out of my league. I was about to travel to do what I loved most and take a huge leap of faith.

I sensed I was on the verge of something huge. I was afraid, but I kept thinking, It will either be a fantastic adventure or a great story, but either way, it will make a good memoir someday.

My mother watched me all the way to the airport gate. She cried, and I cried.

"Are you sure you need to leave? You do not have to go. You don't have to do this, you understand."

"I do, Mom; I have to do this." The part of me that wanted to stay was being destroyed by the dreamer.

Looking back, I can't comprehend how brave it was for my mother to send her often-reckless daughter across the oceans to explore the unknown. However, when it comes to parenting children, she has always emphasized, "Give them roots and wings." And I was about to soar. Both literally and metaphorically.

My brother had handed me an envelope to open during the flight.

"Don't read it until you're in the air," he said, and I dare not break his word. I picked the middle seat and unpacked my Discman, books, and journal for the flight. I took out his message when I was airborne and my ears exploded.

It was a sketch he had made of me when I was about six or seven years old. On the back, he wrote how far this youngster had gone and how far she would go, and he admonished me, above all, to maintain my integrity.

He also attached a fifty-euro bill, despite the fact that he did not have much money. Again, tears spilled down my cheeks. Knowing he believed in me felt like donning a parachute. Either I'd be able to do what I set out to do, or I'd safely return home on the love he'd always given me.

As I stepped onto Vancouver's jet bridge, the summer heat smacked me like a left hand to the face. I had that cactus-like prickly feeling that comes with traveling for so long, and I was even more fatigued from staying up late the night before I went conversing with my new lover, Fergal.

I stood in a long immigration line, waiting to be questioned.

I always feel a little criminal when I walk up to the booth, where some strict woman or guy is waiting to question me about all of my terrible intentions to ruin Gotham City—or Vancouver, as the case may be. And now I'm scared I mistakenly slipped a honey-glazed ham into my suitcase. As I fumble through my responses, growing increasingly clammy and apprehensive, I notice every side eye and lingering time on the computer.

Lo and behold, I fled, imaginary ham and all, and proceeded to the baggage claim, where I would meet my prospective roommates, whom I had found online. Fergal quipped that they could be serial murders, which was amusing in the sense that it could be real. Fortunately for me, they did not appear to be, as they greeted me with smiles and hugs and took me to their car.

I could have ended up anywhere because research was not my strong suit at this moment—or, perhaps, at any point in my life. But somehow I had ended up in Kitsilano, a posh, safe neighborhood of the city. We pulled up and proceeded down to a dark basement apartment with only a few pieces of furniture. It was the ideal humble home for yourselves for the following twelve months.

I awoke the next morning eager to explore my new surroundings, smiling to myself all the way. My roommates hadn't killed me in my sleep, thus the world was my oyster! Becky, everything's coming up! I thought in my best Milhouse tone.

As I walked up the street to acquire groceries, my head bobbled from side to side, as it does when one is overjoyed, grateful, hopeful, and in love. It felt like everything was possible, as if the cosmos, God, or whatever is in control of all of this was preparing me for victory.

My cousin, Kev, just happened to be in town that day. His optimism reminded me of my father's, and Kev embraced the concept of pursuing a dream. He was an immigrant himself, having arrived in Canada about twenty years before. Now he was married with a child, a nice big house, and a respectable job.

Though there was a significant age difference between Kev and me, one huge enough that he could legitimately be my father, we were kindred spirits: two renegades who had abandoned the nest in search of the promised worms.

It took a few days before I identified the location of the wrestling school that Scotty Mac had talked about. Traveling by rail, bus, hand foot and navigating a new transit system was hazardous. It rained as it was in Ireland, soaking the bottoms of my pants and running mascara down my face.

I eventually showed up at the door, looking like a crazed Irish banshee who had followed Scotty across the pond. He must have been startled. But Canadians will be Canadians, so he welcomed me with wide arms, inviting me to join the class despite my rain-soaked jeans.

As we rolled around, exchanging holds and techniques, I felt an instant camaraderie with the other trainees. It seemed like I had discovered my new wrestling family, which was reinforced when they invited me to lunch at Subway.

Over footlongs and Diet Cokes, I listened to tales of the promotion's most notorious figures. With names like Ladies' Choice, El Phantasmo, and Moondog Manson, I couldn't wait to meet these people—and I wouldn't have to wait long. They had a performance coming up that weekend that they were confident they could hire me for.

ECCW didn't have many women, as was customary at the time, but there was one lady I could wrestle, though everyone referred to her as "the drizz" (short for "drizzling shits," i.e., horrible, really bad). Challenge accepted. My goal (which I still have) is to make anyone I share a ring with seem beautiful. That, to me, is the sign of a highly experienced professional wrestler. It is what all greats do really well.

It is especially important to me because women's wrestling is still in its infancy in terms of favorable positioning, and I believe it is my responsibility to improve everyone with whom I interact in the ring so that the sport may continue to thrive.

With this philosophy, or simply my joyful existence, I was booked. I was preparing to make my Canadian debut.

CHAPTER 6

JAPAN

I boarded my Japan Airlines aircraft in Vancouver and met Natalya Neidhart, a buddy from ECCW, at the gate. For all my confidence in North America, uncertainty greeted me at the gate like an old friend.

My dream was to wrestle in Japan, just like all of my heroes. What if I am not ready? What if it is too soon? What happens if I mess it up and fall flat on my face? What if I cannot keep up? Sure, I thought I was the best female wrestler on my circuit, but those women over there were on another level.

I scribbled continuously in my journal throughout the twelve-hour flight to Narita Airport, trying to give myself pep talks and reminding myself that everything would be fine. When the fear began to cripple me, I would look at the time remaining on the journey and tell myself, "Okay, you have eight more hours to be nervous." You're secure now, and that will relax me for the next five to ten minutes.

We landed in Tokyo with just a single problem. We didn't have a visa.

We had to pretend we were tourists because the company we worked for did not provide work licenses. Here came the feeling of being a complete criminal again, similar to smuggling a ham.

We approached the customs table, where stern inspectors were methodically scrutinizing foreigners' bags. My bright pink championship belt was in there, providing no more indication that we hadn't just come to taste the sushi.

If they found out we were coming to work without a visa, we could be booted out of the country. Barred for life. Put in jail. The dream, like the revolution, would end before it began.

They delved into the luggage with great zeal, hand probing relentlessly through all compartments and crevices while I watched, laughing and trying to keep my cool. I'm saying some Hail Marys in my thoughts and at least one round of "Our Father." They somehow missed the championship belt, either through a wonderful miracle or my divine prayer. I smiled at them as if everything was normal, while internally fist-pumping the air and performing a happy dance. This gal isn't going to Japanese jail.

We strolled out to the arrivals hall to meet Shima, a skinny, serious-looking Japanese man wearing spectacles and a high-necked trench coat. He had the standoffish attitude of a man who should not be fucked with.

He escorted us to a black SUV, his menacing demeanor having no effect as I smiled so wide that my tiny mouth felt like it was attached to my forehead. I remained happily gobsmacked as I peered out the window at Tokyo's skyscrapers and brilliant lights.

Shima, evidently amused by my excitement, even smirked occasionally as I cooed over the Land of the Rising Sun. He even complimented me, saying I resembled Britney Spears. I didn't, but I was a young Caucasian female with blond highlights, and one Japanese bartender I met en way said that all white girls have the same face.

We pulled up to a stunning, elegant hotel in the electronics district.

The accommodations, while huge and modern, disappointed me in a manner. I had watched movies and documentaries about tiny, cramped Tokyo hotel rooms, and darn it, I wanted the complete Japanese experience! Even if it meant sleeping in a cramped hotel room. Unfortunately, I would have to make do with my full-sized room, complete with nice, scary toilets.

The next day, I got out of bed early, too energized for jet lag. It was our first major performance in the famed Korakuen Hall.

Wrestling here was a rite of passage for anyone who considered themselves a wrestler's wrestler, which is what I aspired to be. All of my favorite matches have taken place here, including Dynamite Kid versus Tiger Mask, Kobashi versus Misawa, and many more.

Here I was. Rebecca Knox. Only four years ago, there were much too many blond beauties to look at. Tonight, they would all be looking.

I entered the arena, taking care to be attentive of every move I took. This was the step that Eddie Guerrero and Terry Funk had taken. Mick Foley got ready in the locker room. I climbed the stairs leading to the main hall. Everyone who had ever performed there had left their signatures on the gray wall. It was like wrestling's equivalent of the Hollywood Walk of Fame, but on a tight budget.

After standing bewildered and almost star-struck in front of the wall for what seemed like hours, I signed my name among some of the greatest legends to ever grace a wrestling ring.

The IWGP roster had an eclectic mix of men and women from all over. Some were legends in their native Mexico and Japan, while others were complete unknowns like myself. Shima, on the other hand, did such an excellent job of promoting me that you'd think I was the biggest celebrity to leave Ireland since Bono. And I felt that way when I stepped out for my first match. I was paired with Nattie in an intergender tag match against two of the Japanese male stars. Despite the name, the International Women's Grand Prix was not a women-only promotion. The males were generous enough to bang around for us and make Nattie and I appear like badasses!

Upon our arrival, the audience bombarded us with streams of ribbon, littering the ring like it was Mardi Gras.

Wrestling in front of a Japanese crowd is completely different from wrestling in front of a Western audience. The Japanese don't yay, boo, or chant in the same way, so it can be disconcerting for a first-timer as they sit there calmly and occasionally clap respectfully as you try to amaze them with your most remarkable moves. I enjoy the challenge—it's similar to wooing someone with an aura of mystery about them. You're not sure if they like you or not.

And I think the Japanese crowd liked us because after the match, ladies rushed the ring with magnificent bouquets of flowers for us.

Wrestling in Japan has already surpassed my high expectations. There was nothing like it.

Shima promised to make me a star. Despite the fact that I couldn't even afford adequate ring gear.

One night in, it was already operational.

"Rebecca-San!" a loud cry erupted from behind me. I turned around to see dozens of fans closing in on me, yelling at the top of their voices as if I were Harry Styles leaving Madison Square Garden in a feathered boa.

What the real fuck?

I was attempting to exit the arena, but they kept approaching from all directions, asking for pictures and signatures, and bringing me gifts. I was no one, but the perception that I was a big deal had whipped these individuals into a frenzy.

I wanted to soak it all in for as long as possible, taking photos with everyone until the gathering became too large and security grabbed me from the pile of admirers and led me to the bus.

My sacrifice of leaving Ireland, my family, and Fergal behind was paying off. I could hardly believe how quickly everything was occurring.

The next day, the press was full of adulation for Rebecca Knox, a champion. I discovered the pot of gold at the end of the rainbow, and it was wrestling in Japan.

However, it appears that after we left Korakuen, I slipped, staggered, and fell, scattering those golden riches, with the pot eventually rebounding and hitting me in the head.

The throngs thinned out over the next two weeks as we traveled across the country. So did my confidence.

Every night, I was put in the main event, teamed up with two wrestling legends, Gran Hamada and Aja Kong, to face Los Brazos, a Mexican trio of muscular brothers who had giggled so hard that a small replica of the Grand Canyon was carved into their foreheads.

Shima wanted me to be a high flier (which I wasn't really good at), so he paired me with Brazo de Platino, who was an outstanding base and would toss me up, catch me, and move me in such a manner that the audience thought I was doing all the effort.

That is one of the illusions of wrestling. Often, credit is given to the flyers when, in reality, the person standing there and making the move is doing the hard work.

Since coming to Canada, I've created a name for myself as a skilled technical, ground-based wrestler. I felt absolutely out of my element in the air. I was afraid. I was a phony, and I knew it. Not being in tune with the group's mood, I vented my emotions to some of the other girls on the trip, who were already irritated by my obvious preferential treatment and main event spot.

I was the show's chosen star. I attracted attention and was brought out on my own for dinners with sponsors—a circumstance peculiar to Japanese celebrity artists, who are frequently treated to costly meals and experiences. It was developing animosity, especially because I wasn't even thankful for it. I'd piss and complain about not being able to wrestle the way I wanted to when I was given everything. Midway through the trip, I realized I had created some enemies.

I lacked courage and humility because I was so young, terrified of failing to fulfill my ambition of wrestling in Japan, and I knew I wasn't especially adept in this new high-flying main event role. Sometimes I did well, but most of the time I failed and Shima chastised me.

"Give 60%, 70%. Not 100 %. You try too hard. You're no good. If you go 60%, you can move up. If you go 100%, you will only go down."

I didn't know how to contribute anything other than my all. Even now, I would never try to deliver anything less than my best.

To be fair to Shima, I am guilty of this observation. I try too hard. I really want to entertain the people who have come to see me and prove to myself and the world that I am the finest. But, ultimately, striving too hard means admitting that you don't fully trust yourself to be good enough yet. And I surely did not do so in Japan right now.

CHAPTER 7

THE HEAT

Despite this brand-new incredible offer, after being scolded so many times by Shima, I felt like I had failed in Japan.

As a result, and in keeping with the brand, I began to push myself even harder. My matches started to get more complex. Now that I had wrestled in Japan (although terribly), I pretended to be better than I was and attempted things I couldn't pull off. I tackled difficult areas without completely understanding the psychology behind them. Nonetheless, faking it until I made it, I continued to generate buzz throughout the world.

Fergal had gone across the country to train at the New Japan dojo in Santa Monica, California. I came to stay for a few weeks in March, hoping to pick up a few things or make a few bookings.

To be honest, I didn't learn much about either.

The dojo was a vast warehouse with a ring, a weights room, showers, a restaurant, and a large padded section. We slept on old mattresses in the attic, which was infested with rats. Fergal, being the tremendous talent that he is, had already established himself in the short time he was there.

Fergal was asked to train in Tokyo as a young child, or apprentice wrestler, a few weeks into my time at the dojo.

When he went, I realized our relationship was coming to an end. The distance was too vast, and during the last few months, I had become demanding, clingy, and afraid of losing him. It didn't matter if it was due to ego, insecurity, or a combination of the two; he was about to realize his dream, and I wasn't going to be a part of that.

He went on to become one of New Japan's top stars and the founder of the Bullet Club, one of wrestling's most popular groups.

But by the time he departed, we scarcely spoke.

I dropped him off at the airport with one of our friends and fellow dojo roommates, Chad Allegra (aka WWE's Karl Anderson), and we didn't even exchange goodbye hugs.

Chad consoled me while I sobbed my eyes out after Fergal left. Too embarrassed to tell Chad the truth, that I was heartbroken by my broken heart and knew that this move meant my and Fergal's relationship was finished, I blamed my frenzy on a family disease.

On the phone, my cousin begged me to return to Canada as I sobbed, "I feel like a part of me just died."

I have always had a flair for the dramatics. But this was my first true love, and I had fucked it up. Now he was leaving me behind forever. When he arrived in Japan and called me a few days later, we agreed that our relationship had ended but that we would always be friends. But, as the band The Script famously sang, "When a heart breaks, no, it doesn't break even"—and I was unquestionably the more distraught.

I returned to Canada, and like any heartbroken adolescent girl, I set my sights on acquiring a better figure. As if it will relieve his suffering and make him want me back.

A company called Ring Angels offered me custom matches in North Carolina, as well as a lingerie photo shoot, for $150, which sounded like a little fortune.

Of course, it contradicted everything I had planned to do. I wanted to prove that I should be judged based on my technical abilities, and I never wanted to sexualize myself for fear of losing my reputation as a wrestler.

I did it anyway.

In my bewilderment, sadness, and desire to reach the top and feel good about myself, I rationalized, "All WWE girls do it; it's just part of the job."

I despised it. I despised every second of it. Trying to fit into the mold I had sworn to reject felt like selling my soul for $150. I still grimace every time I see those photos—this puffy, awkward nineteen-year-old attempting to appear seductive yet clearly uncomfortable. Being a woman in wrestling may be quite complicated. This is especially true if you were raised Catholic. You see what women on TV are doing and think that's how you move ahead, but you don't want to be objectified, so you question if you should abandon your femininity entirely. It's a fine disorienting balance to walk carefully when it should be simple. Simply be yourself and do what you love well. But instead of learning that I didn't have to market myself as a gorgeous little sex kitten, I focused more on my physique. As if that were the only thing that could propel me to success.

I halved my calorie intake and increased my workout intensity. It wasn't long before I noticed significant changes in my body, my attitude (not for the better), and my complete obsession with the physical.

In the midst of my identity crisis, my Canadian visa was about to expire, and if I didn't find a way to stay, I would have to return to Ireland, where I had told my mother I would go back to college. The hourglass was running out, and I couldn't stop the sand from falling.

I departed Vancouver with a sorrowful heart. Much had transpired in that single year. I had evolved and matured in numerous ways. I had reached and fulfilled all of my aspirations on that first night in Japan, but then I began to slip hopelessly downward, believing my own trash far too rapidly.

I had done the things I had promised not to do, and with it came new insecurities that quickly consumed me while I floundered at home, desperately looking for methods to make it to the big time before the summer was out.

Or certainly before I turned twenty. Because after that, I decided that I was too old. I needed to be seen as the teenage protégée I was and get signed by one of the bigger companies, such as WWE or, more preferably, TNA, where they place a greater emphasis on women's wrestling, while I was still nineteen, or, to be honest, before Fergal did, so that I could validate myself as worthy and make him want me back.

I returned to Ireland, now living under my mother's roof, and she was forcing me to make a plan based on my prior pledge to her.

I didn't have one, but I planned to get autographed. But that wasn't practical enough and she did not want me out there slinging pillows at another woman in a G-string.

CHAPTER 8

THE FALSE FINISH

Italy had become a hotbed for wrestling, with some events attracting up to ten thousand people, so when I was invited on a tour, despite my existential crisis, I jumped at the chance.

I stepped off the airport into the oppressive summer heat and was directed to the tour bus, where two kind Canadian faces emerged from under navy bus seat cushions.

"Hi! "I'm Kevin!"

"Hi! I'm Rami!"

Kevin and Rami, also known as Kevin Steen and El Generico, or Kevin Owens and Sami Zayn, would go on to become two of WWE's most popular wrestlers and WrestleMania main eventers.

But back then, they were just two best friends with a fan base on the indie circuit, bantering back and forth like a couple of old hens, and they were gracious enough to include me in their friend group.

My opponent never showed up, leaving me as the sole woman, leaving no choice but to throw me in a match against Kevin and Rami. Two of the best wrestlers in the world took me through some barn burners, even if no one was watching.

The buildings could hold between 5,000 and 10,000 people. Our best night gathered a maximum of 100 individuals. And even that is a stretch.

What the promoter failed to grasp was that advertising was an important component of enticing people to attend an event, as did having some major names who people would pay money to see. We weren't major worldwide draws at the time. Yes, Kevin and Rami were well-known on the indies, but to draw large crowds, wrestlers who had previously appeared on television were preferred.

In between shows, I binged on cereal and threw up frequently without trying to hide it, passing it off as drinking contaminated tap water.

Even though I was hurting mentally and physically, Kevin and Rami provided solace for my broken heart. The two of them, who had been traveling the world together for years, acted like a funny old married couple, delighting everyone on the roster with a 24-hour sitcom.

Though the tour had not been a success in traditional terms, and I was exhausted from wrestling and vomiting incessantly, I was sad to leave my newfound buddies.

I still had one more weekend of bookings before heading to Orlando.

I arrived at a location in Germany, a little thicker than usual, and was greeted by Doug Williams, one of the UK's most respected wrestlers. "No more abs?" he inquired, as if I were not a teenage girl with a complex. More tone deaf than malevolent.

"No, Doug." I wanted to declare, "I had a fucking eating disorder and was killing myself."

But instead, I chuckled and said, "Ha-ha, apparently not," before crying in the restroom.

My opponent was as green as goose dung, but I wasn't about to tone it down for anyone longer. I'd wrestled internationally, created a name for myself, completed multiple tours of Japan, and was a regular main eventer.

I had the X-factor. Someone on MySpace told me this.

We were having the match I wanted, and it was going to be fantastic. Whether my opponent appreciated it or not. Alternatively, whether she realized what she was doing or not. My earlier goal of making everyone appear good had been reduced to only wanting to make myself look nice.

However, on this fateful night, I made no one seem good!

She didn't know what she was doing.

The end outcome is...

We went out there and stunk up every complicated area we tried.

After one botch too many, the audience began chanting, "Women's wrestling."

If the crowd chants "Women's wrestling," it is meant as the highest compliment. Back then, it was considered the sharpest of insults.

In a rage, I grabbed the girl and tried an outstanding modified version of a German suplex. She clung to me for dear life, terrified and unable to understand what was going on, falling right on my eye. The only thing amazing about my attempted maneuver was how much blood poured out from above my eye.

Almost soon, I lost vision in my left eye. It appeared that the entire globe was covered with crimson paint.

I was irritated with her for being so incompetent that she put me in this situation, but it was my fault for striving too hard. Even at nineteen, I was a veteran, and I should have known better.

I ended the match with blood flowing down my face and was taken to the hospital right away.

I sustained a concussion, and the huge gash above my eye required stitches.

My main concern was how to hide the injuries from my mother. She was already looking for me to leave wrestling. If I arrived home looking like Frankenstein, she would go insane.

Dieting too hard had sapped all of my energy, especially since I was also wrestling. On my rigorous calorie-deficient diet, I wouldn't be able to grow muscle or look as ripped as I desired, therefore I wouldn't have gotten WWE's notice as a body girl with wrestling skills. And I didn't believe I could contribute anything to the TNA roster in my current state of competence. My plans had already failed.

I wasn't sure what I wanted. I did not want the pressure. I didn't want to risk failure. I didn't want to experience agony. I didn't want to be unclear about what was going to happen next.

What I did know was that I lacked the courage to tell anyone I was hurting.

Like a coward, I used the injury as an excuse to walk away while I tried to work out my head, rather than admitting that I couldn't do it.

A doctor friend provided me with a reasonable excuse, something that sounded serious but could be reversed if I changed my mind: "damage to the eighth cranial nerve," which is essentially tinnitus but sounds quite gruesome.

At the very least, this would give me some time to figure out the world, but my mind was so muddled that I had no notion which way to go. Only a year ago, it seemed so straightforward and obvious.

I left for Orlando anyhow, an unpredictable mess.

I was connecting through New York when I experienced an epiphany. Or a panic attack. Maybe anything in-between.

Wrestling was over. I was finished. I needed to come home.

I was going to contact my mother and tell her right now. She'd be overjoyed to see me again and learn that I was leaving wrestling to become the daughter she desired.

I found the nearest pay phone at the airport and phoned. Prepared to stay on the straight and narrow. I'm ready to finally make her pleased with my decision.

"Mom, I do not want to do this. I want to come home."

"No." Her voice was clear and without hesitancy.

Huh? It was the last thing I expected to hear.

She didn't want me to wrestle. She didn't want me to diet or train obsessively. How could she say no to this? Especially considering it was the first time she'd heard it. Had she expected that I would back out?

The panic grew. I just need her to know I am real.

"I understand I've been all over the place. I apologize. I can't do it. I will obtain a regular job. I'll return to college. Please. I will be normal. I promise to be normal. I just want to come home."

"You have dropped out of everything and haven't followed through. You can't do it this time."

My heart fell. My stomach constricted; tears streamed down my cheeks; my voice strained.

"Please, Mom, please. I do not want to be like this anymore," I begged and begged.

"I'm sorry."

She hung up, leaving me in a state of dread. Lost, alone, broken, and feeling like an absolute failure. I had wasted my life in the pursuit of abs. For the sake of fitting into a mold and becoming more deserving of my ambitions. The dreams I had were already on their way to fulfillment.

Passers-by glanced at me with pity and concern as I made my way to the gate, face crimson and snot falling.

I waddled aboard my aircraft to Orlando with sunk shoulders and found my seat, ravenous and with just a big bag of raw oats to eat for whatever stupid reason.

After what seemed like an unending day of travel, I finally arrived at my new home in Orlando. There were students everywhere, loud music playing, and annoying frat males hanging from the stairwells. I rushed past them to find my flat. Brown walls and brown furnishings all sit on a brown carpet.

After crawling into bed that night, under my sheet, which offered about as much heat as a sleeve of newspaper, and resting my head on a cheap pillow, I alternated between sensations of anxiety, melancholy, and dread.

I called my mother the next day to tell her I had arrived safely.

She had a wrath in her voice that she saved for rare occasions. On this special occasion, she came upon the lingerie shoot I had done in North Carolina.

"You are acting like a porn star. You need to appreciate yourself. What will you do with your life? Are you going to be a 40-year-old wrestler who lives in a trailer park?"

I had no more rebuttals or fury; I was defeated and ashamed of myself. And she had seen the lingerie shot that did not wind up in a pornographic magazine.

The brown walls were closing in, and I couldn't see a better life ahead of me. All I had was this personal-training diploma to help me get back on track, but it felt terrible.

What I rapidly realized in personal-training school was that as much as I enjoyed training myself for the sake of vanity, I couldn't care less about teaching anyone else. The class was uninteresting, and the workouts were simple. I had no incentive to succeed and quickly learnt the difference between a genuine enthusiasm and a contrived one.

I rely on my roommates for rides to and from school, but I am otherwise tied to the brown flat and sitting on the brown couch, with just dinner preparation and dreams of happier days to keep me occupied.

My golden years were behind me. At nineteen, I was a washed-up has-been.

CHAPTER 9

NEW SCHOOL

In February 2007, I came home with my diploma, feeling low, meek, and insecure. At the very least, I had stayed with it.

I hit the Dublin pavements looking for work, wearing a forced smile to hide the fact that I was dying within. I was a considerable way from the main events at Korakuen Hall and was being pursued by swarms of spectators.

My mother had been struggling with the decision to accept a severance payment from Aer Lingus, where she had worked for twenty-nine years.

Chris had taken a similar package two years before, and she was divided between enjoying a leisurely life with her new husband and continuing to do the work she still enjoyed. And make no mistake: she adored it in the same way that I used to love wrestling.

She was at the top of the flight attendant food chain in terms of experience and rank, as well as cabin manager, or the primary eventer for flight attendants. She took delight in establishing a happy atmosphere for everyone she worked with.

"It trickles down from the top," she explained.

Finally, she decided to marry and spend time with her husband.

As she was printing her resignation, a thought occurred to her.

"Would you like me to hand in your résumé?"

"Sure, you might as well," I replied casually. Without my own dreams, I might as well follow hers.

I arrived at my interview primped and primed, wearing high heels, pearl earrings, and a bright pink blazer.

Who was I?

A flight attendant, I suppose....

I landed the job.

Desperate for a community similar to what I had discovered in wrestling, and in search of a new passion, I experimented with professions and hobbies as if they were scenes from a rom-com. I worked at a Pilates studio—it was too bland! English was taught as a foreign language—too detailed! I took capoeira classes, and there were too many patterns! I took Muay Thai classes, and they were quite unpleasant!

I did a bodybuilding competition with only three weeks of preparation time—too short! Though I finished third, it was as insipid as I expected. My awful posing routine to Shawn Michaels' entrance music, in my cheap red bikini, while lathered in a chocolate-like coating of fake tan, is why I'm glad iPhones weren't in the hands of everyone on the planet in 2008. Furthermore, an audience member's remark that "the third-place winner was too fat" was disturbing. Especially given that I was already bulimic.

I needed to find the proper fit. Something comfortable but with a little flavor, perhaps something elastic to allow for growth. Then I saw it! The Gaiety School of Acting offers a ten-week acting class! I'd have the opportunity to express myself, perform, and possibly regain some confidence. It was the best fit! I put it on and twirled while my pals applauded and yelled as I strutted around like a tiger. I could get into this shit.

After one game of Zip Zap Zop, I was ready to quit my good, pensionable work, withdraw all of my life savings, and return to school with a group of theater kids. My mother, on the other hand, was less enthusiastic about my revelation.

American schools were #1 on my list. I hoped that if I could get over there, I'd be able to be anyone I wanted to be, rather than this insecure strange wreck. More significantly, I would not have to answer to my mother.

The benefit of being a flight attendant paid off when I scheduled my first audition at a New York school called the American Academy of Dramatic Arts for an overnight the following week.

As soon as we landed, I threw my uniform on the floor of my hotel room and dashed to school, my knees smacking together as I hurried down Madison Avenue. I arrived at the enormous redbrick building, which had an outstanding list of alumni, including Robert Redford and Paul Rudd. As I waited outside the audition room, I attempted in vain to fan the pit stains out of my shirt.

Either I take a step in the correct direction and create the life I want to live, or I'm told I'm the shits and return to my unfulfilled life. It all hinged on this one audition.

I had carefully chosen a speech that would capitalize on my unshakable nervousness.

After that, the judge sat silent for the longest fifteen seconds of my life. It was like watching The X Factor and being either blown away or told not to show your face in public again.

"That was wonderful," he remarked finally, and my insides skipped like a schoolchild.

Holy fuck! Maybe not everything is lost, I reasoned as I exhaled in relief and silently praised the brilliant playwright whose words managed to make me appear good at this critical juncture in my life.

"Tell me, why do you want to act?"

I had never truly considered why I like performing. It just drew something out of me.

"Well, I became a professional wrestler at the age of fifteen, but I quit over three years ago and have been feeling a hole ever since. I believe that nothingness is an artistic expression. I want to create. I want to perform. "I want to live in another head and body that does not feel like mine."

He considered my response for a moment before advising, "Do not tell yourself that you cannot do it. If it isn't for you, others will tell you.

(I understand that he intended this as a motivational tool against self-destruction. But people warned me I wouldn't main event WrestleMania, so we'll get to it.

"I'd like you to pursue this. I am offering you a position in the program and our highest scholarship."

My eyes started to moisten.

"Thank you, thank you so much."

I left stunned, alternating between wide-eyed awe, sobbing, and joyfully fist-pumping the air.

Maybe I can trust myself again. Walking through the streets of Manhattan, a location that had always fascinated me as a six-year-old, I got a sense I hadn't had in a while. I thought that anything was possible. You simply need to believe in yourself again.

Returning to Ireland with an offer from a prominent acting school changed my mother's perspective on my unorthodox goals. Maybe I wasn't all dog shit. Maybe, by some miracle, I did have a spark of talent.

I had saved every bit I could while working in the airline for just this type of chance.

Even with the grant, living in New York City for the two years of the course without a work visa was still prohibitively expensive, therefore I did not participate in the program. And, while I would have to change my plans, the most difficult obstacle—my mother's disapproval—had been overcome, and I felt like I was now open to a world of possibilities.

CHAPTER 10

THE COMEBACK

When I graduated from college and entered the real world, auditions were few, and obtaining an agent was like mining for diamonds. Surprisingly, no one wanted to take a chance on this absolutely normal person with no experience beyond her college degree—something I hadn't expected. Still, I hit the pavement, bringing my résumé and headshot to every game and gig in town.

With no acting employment on the horizon, I decided it was time to make my New York plans and book my flights.

But, as luck would have it, weeks before my trip to New York, I received a call from Vikings, a new show that had begun filming in Ireland. It was one of the largest TV productions Ireland has ever hosted, and they wanted me to be a part of it!

However, this was not a job for which I was prepared. I was asked to join the stunt crew. My résumé featured a plethora of bizarre athletic experiences I had accumulated over the years while looking for a hobby to replace wrestling, including my abilities to horseback ride, sword fight, ski, and scuba dive, as well as my experience with Muay Thai and bodybuilding. They assumed the physical jack-of-all-trades was a stuntwoman.

"We might have some work for you on set here," Paul Burke, the stunt coordinator, suggested. "Would you be interested?"

"Absolutely I would be!" I accepted as soon as I realized I wasn't a stuntwoman.

Sure, that was not acting. But it was acting adjacent, and I couldn't afford to mess this one up.

Okay, brain! Think! How will you pull this off? You were a good wrestler. Go to Joe's school to brush up. Then use that confidence to your stunt job! Bing bang boom! Nobody will notice a thing!

I arrived at a beginner's lesson feeling less scared than I typically am in similar situations. I wasn't wrestling anymore, and the purpose wasn't the same, so who cared if I messed up?

Joe's ease of coaching calmed whatever remaining nerves I had. He is a natural leader, an alpha who is communicative, polite, and considerate; nonetheless, you must not cross him.

We started locking up and moving around, doing drills with tackles and headlocks.

"You still got it," Joe began to mock and yell at me.

I glowed like a New York Christmas tree.

Joe grabbed me aside after class. "Would you ever consider going to a WWE tryout? You clearly still enjoy it."

I felt transported to another dimension. My body screamed at me with a deep sense that could not be ignored. YES! I yelled in my own head.

Externally, I could not say that was what I wanted to accomplish. So, after staring at him for what seemed like hours, I said, "Ah, thanks, Joe, but I already have my plan; I'm heading to New York, visas and tickets are booked, and I want to pursue this acting thing. And I suppose this stunt stuff now."

"Well, think about it, 'cause I think you'd get it."

I didn't have to think about it. I knew this was correct. After six years of pushing, I finally felt like I was being pushed.

A few days later, after much self-talk, coming to Jesus, and finally being honest with myself, I realized I needed to postpone all of my future goals.

I called Joe. "I think I might take you up on getting that tryout."

"Excellent, I'll give Robbie Brookside a call."

Robbie Brookside?! I adored Robbie Brookside. I just met him once, but he was the type of person that made you feel like you'd known him forever. And now Robbie was on WWE's recruiting squad.

"Knoxy giiiiiirl!" he exclaimed, his thick Liverpool accent sounding like an angelic siren in my ear.

"Hey, Robbie! So glad to hear from you!"

"I was wondering what happened to you. I recall that young girl who went head to head with Sweet Saraya. What have you been up to?"

"Oh, everything, Robbie, but I was never able to get wrestling out of my system."

"Well, I'd love for you to come and try this. We'll host a three-day tryout in Birmingham in five weeks. If you could send me some images and a résumé, I'll forward them to the appropriate people."

"Absolutely! I'll send that over right away," I said gleefully.

Finally, I was determined to get the deal.

My training increased and my diet tightened as I prepared for not one, but two major opportunities.

I still had my role on Vikings. With 4:00 a.m. wake-up calls, twelve-hour days, long trips to and from set, and a gym stop on the way home, I was in my element.

The production was massive. The actors were cool, and the stunt performers were competent. If I wanted, I could keep performing this stunt. But I needed to see what life was like in WWE and if it was truly my calling.

However, telling my mother that I was returning to wrestling would not be easy.

"They heard about me and asked if I wanted to try out. "I'd like to give it a shot," I informed her. It was more of a diversion of the truth than a clear lie.

She was remarkably calm. The notion of being recruited by the world's largest and most recognized wrestling organization sounded more appealing than "Hey, Mom, I'm going to Luxembourg for the weekend to wrestle in a field for free."

Besides, I had proven to her that I could do whatever I set my mind to. I completed my college degree. Perhaps I might demonstrate to her that I have the potential to make an impact in the wrestling business. Change how women's wrestling was seen, ushering in a new era.

I packed my luggage, dressed in my best exercise gear, and arrived at Dublin Airport prepared to earn my way into the world's largest wrestling promotion.

I located the nearest ATM and withdrew a few euros to get me through the next few days. When I checked my account, there was just thirty-five euros remaining. Welp. I laughed to myself since I had nothing to lose but everything to gain. I should make this work.

CHAPTER 11

THE CONTRACT SIGNING

Four weeks after the tryout, on my way to the gym, I received a call from an American number. "Hi, Rebecca, it's Canyon."

I pulled over to the side of the road, expecting to hear either the best or the worst news of my life.

"I'm delighted I'm the one to call you, because I know how much this means to you. We would like to offer you a developmental position at NXT with a tentative start date of July 2013.

Tears streamed down my face. Butterflies performed a sophisticated, synchronized dance routine in my belly. My voice rose to octaves it had never reached before as I squeaked, "Thank you so much! "I will not let you down!" I was overwhelmed with gratitude and wanted nothing more than to make them glad that they had trusted me.

By the time I got to the gym, I was too excited to concentrate.

"Gah, my god!! Don't tell anyone, but I just got signed!" I beam at one of my pals who happened to be present. "I want to make women's wrestling the coolest thing on television! I am telling you now, man. I am going to be the main event at WrestleMania!" I was overjoyed as I leaped up and down and spun in circles.

"Ha-ha-ha. That's great! And it's fine to have dreams, Becky, but be realistic," he responded in the most non-offensive way imaginable.

It may sound strange to have a friend shit all over your dreams so casually, but it truly wasn't. At the time, it seemed nearly impossible to have women as the main event of WrestleMania. But he said I couldn't, so I had to.

All I had to do was wrap myself in bubble wrap until July and I'd be able to start at WWE's brand-new state-of-the-art training facility in Orlando, known as the Performance Center.

Joe had already left for Florida to begin training, but things had not gone well. A few days in, he had already sustained a concussion and was struggling to adjust to his new lifestyle.

A trainee's daily existence included a laundry list of manners and regulations. Joe made sure to give me the rundown so I wouldn't get off to a horrible start:

"Shake everyone's hands. You must ride with the girls. It looks horrible to ride with the guys. Do not become engaged with any of the lads. They frown on such things."

"They dislike those who have previous experience. They believe they are uncoachable. Be coachable."

"To protect yourself in the ring, keep your hands up at all times."

"Never talk back, even if they're wrong—just say, 'Yes, sir, won't happen again,' and move on."

The list went on and on, and I clung to each word, hoping to make the best first impression possible while not offending anyone. I had also taken years off from wrestling and wanted to be regarded as a blank canvas, but after years of refining your profession, being told you know nothing felt like a mental fuck. However, I had already decided that no matter how many tests they put at me, I would not let them break my spirit.

I packed my stuff and caught the plane to Florida. This time was very different from the previous ill-planned Orlando trip. This time, I knew exactly what I was doing. I was about to revolutionize wrestling forever.

CHAPTER 12

NXT

Grandma remarked, "I hope all your dreams come true," and it felt like she was schmoozing Jesus every day she was up there. After years of pondering, fretting, and wondering, What if...? I was here in Orlando, eager to start at NXT and see if I had what it takes.

The most important thing for me was not to fuck everything up. Which was quite likely, given that I always keep a bright red self-destruct button at the forefront of my consciousness.

Joe suggested that I wear a "nice dress" on the big first day. Apparently, all the girls wore "nice dresses." But I didn't own any lovely dresses. I had no dresses at all. And definitely not a lot of money to spend on "nice dresses."

He took me to Ross Dress for Less, where I purchased three outfits for the grand total of $30.

Not being well-versed in the art of nice-dress buying, I had acquired three frumpy bridesmaid-looking dresses. You know, the kind that a bride buys for her friends to ensure that they do not overshadow her.

I chose the best one and hung it up for the morning. A lovely, frilly, beige fucker. Who could resist me at this level of high fashion? They might send me to the main roster right immediately! I thought.

I got up early, unable to sleep due to the excitement, and spent hours precisely straightening my hair and ensuring my makeup looked as well as I was capable of.

It was all for naught. When I stepped into the humid Orlando air, my hair frizzy and my makeup spilled down my face.

Great.

I could scarcely speak during the ten-minute journey from our place. As we reached the warehouse, I noticed a large sign on the building that read "WWE PERFORMANCE CENTER."

This was exactly how I imagined a wrestling school to look eleven years ago, when I took my first class in that small school hall in Bray with six padded mats on the floor.

Joe and I entered the front entrance, where friendly office staff greeted us excitedly and issued us official badges complete with lanyards. Ryan Katz, a bald man wearing a colorful suit and sporting the world's largest smile, conducted a guided tour of the structure. He was a member of the creative team and shined as he escorted us through the building. "This is HHH's baby," he announced. HHH—aka Hunter Hearst Helmsley, aka Paul Levesque—was one of WWE's biggest stars and the reason every youngster and teen in the late 1990s got in trouble at school for saying, "Suck it!" while gesticulating at their crotch. He was well-known for his amusing performance with his popular group, or "faction" in wrestling terms—DX—but he was also one of WWE's most adaptable characters, effortlessly transitioning from comedy to badass. He has recently been tasked with overseeing talent development. He was Vince McMahon's son-in-law and was expected to eventually oversee the entire organization.

And his infant was spotless. Freshly painted walls, unstained carpets, and no dust in sight; it seemed as if the entire place had been doused with new-car scent. The walls were plastered with portraits of icons such as Dusty Rhodes, Vince McMahon Sr., Harley Race, Gorgeous George, Mae Young, and Bruno Sammartino.

The facility included a cutting-edge gym, a physio room, a practice area with seven wrestling rings, a promo room, a green-screen room, a kitchen, televisions, and the most magnificent locker rooms and restrooms I'd ever seen in a sporting venue.

After a long and winding trek, I arrived at the wrestling Mecca. If you wanted to be successful in this industry, here was the place to be.

I felt completely out of place.

This was especially true given that I was about to face a direct competitor. An all-talented meeting was about to take place on the gym floor, conducted by the head coach, Bill DeMott, who I had seen tear individuals to bits on Tough Enough years before.

As I entered the crowd, any semblance of confidence I had gained throughout my tryout was utterly gone. I started comparing my drab, awkward self to the other female newbies, who happened to be the most beautiful and glamorous group of women I'd ever seen, replete with sparkling, compelling personalities.

The new surge of guys were built like massive stone statues and had to turn sideways to pass through the doors.

When I thought I couldn't be any more insecure, the seasoned trainees joined us. They were all equally impressive and radiant, as if their blood was solely composed of charisma.

If you had to pick one person on that day in July 2013 who you knew was not going to make it, it would have been me.

It didn't help that DeMott began the meeting with an ominous warning.

"Look at the folks beside you. They will most likely not make it."

It appeared like the entire group had turned to look squarely at the strange person in the bridesmaid's outfit.

When the group returned their focus to the front, Bill, who was cordial in the "I will slit your throat and not think twice about it but also tell you a joke while I do it" type of way, introduced us to the rest of the coaching team. The mere thought of these guys as my future coaches made my brain explode with admiration.

Dusty Rhodes, the famed wrestler, would serve as our promo (promotional interview) coach. He, a mold-breaker and one of the greatest promoters of all time, suddenly dressed like the charming yet sassy old man he had transformed into. He wore ill-fitting blue trousers tucked into work boots, a baseball cap, spectacles, and a baggy T-shirt that didn't quite cover his elbows, which sagged from years of bumping and elbowing people on the top of their heads. I quickly sought his approval.

There was the "Red Rooster" Terry Taylor, who told me that before I departed, TNA (where he had worked) considered hiring me. This provided reassurance while also calling into question the previous seven years.

There was Billy Gunn of the legendary tag team The New Age Outlaws, who was even larger in person. He shook my hand as if he intended to break it.

Joey Mercury was best known as one half of the tag team MNM or J&J Security, which worked for a hot kid named Seth Rollins. Joey was also regarded as one of the top wrestling minds. A savant, nearly. And he had a serious stroke. Despite his diminutive stature, he was the most terrifying member of the crew. I was too terrified to say hello.

There was Nick Dinsmore, also known as Eugene, the cognitively stunted wrestling sensation. He spoke in a dry and friendly tone.

There was Norman Smiley, whom I had met at my tryout and already adored.

Then there was Sara Amato, the women's head coach and the person I was most dreading seeing. Fuck. She accompanied me on my first tour of Japan. That time I was the main attraction, treated like royalty while still behaving like a moany bitch. Hell, she was definitely at both of the SHIMMER exhibitions I missed.

What if she harbors a grudge? What if she assumes I believed I was above learning from her? What if she dislikes me?

I envisioned her inner monologue being a diatribe about how bad I am and how I got through the holes. How the heck did this woman get here? She hasn't wrestled in years, yet she's still in WWE? That's ridiculous! She wasn't very good back then!

She would have been correct to feel that way.

I shook her hand, not wanting to appear overly friendly with any of the instructors.

"Oh, hey, it's been a while," she responded casually, with what I believe was a side-eye.

It's official: she believes I shouldn't be here.

The guilt was crushing. Who was I to abandon the thing that had given me so much for so long and waltz in here and take the keys to the kingdom while everyone else had been suffering for years?

I was the prodigal son. And I absolutely despise the Prodigal Son narrative. Bitch gets to spend all of his money, live frivolously, and do anything he wants before strutting back in as if nothing happened, while his brother worked and remained loyal the entire time. And the dad just says, "No worries, fam—we good," and gives him whatever else he wants! If I were that good brother, I would be furious. And if I'm one of those good wrestlers who has been committed and true to the grind, I'm quite upset.

The wrestling community is a little hamlet, so I knew many of the folks who had made it this far.

CHAPTER 13

THE HOPE SPOT

The nickname "Black Friday" circulated around the Performance Center. No, the cutbacks were not in item prices, but in contracts.

Every now and then, on a random Friday, people on the chopping block were summoned to the office and informed that their dream had come to an end. It never became less gloomy. Not only would you lose the people who had grown like family to you in this wild circus, but it would also serve as a reminder of the dream's vulnerability. That it may be over in an instant at the whim of someone else.

I was in the middle of a training session on Friday following my huge live event debut when one of my pals, Frenchy, alias Tom La Ruffa, approached me.

"What are you going to do?" he asked in his heavy French accent.

"About what?"

"I'm so sorry, Becky. Didn't you hear? Joe has been released."

Joe had become my brother. Every night after training, I would cry on his shoulder. He was the pick-me-up I needed when I was down; he reminded me that at the end of the day, no matter how awful things are, if you have a friend to come home to who can make you smile, everything would be fine.

He was also incredibly gifted, and had something unique to offer. He would defend what he believed in and thought was correct. As a result, he antagonized the wrong people at the wrong time.

I returned to our filthy apartment to find him lounging in the brown recliner he had just purchased a week before. He smiled at me with his trademark Joe smile, warm and playful at the same time.

"How are you feeling?"

"Relieved, to be honest."

At the very least, it made one of us. I fell into tears while hugging him.

It was a sad ending for foreigners like Joe and myself. We'd uprooted our lives, spent all of our earnings on starting up a shop and paying off our visas to live here, and it could all be gone in a second, leaving you with the weight of rejection and no money in your pocket. It's the price you pay for the opportunity to realize your ambitions.

Now I was alone. I was broke. I had no idea how I was going to live; I just knew I would. Despite all odds, I'd make it.

In the calm of the night, I'd dream of better days ahead. Some days felt effortless, as if my work wasn't at stake. Days when I made it to the main roster. Days when I was the main event at WrestleMania. It all seemed so impossible, but I was the only one living in my thoughts, and it was great to inject some optimism between periods of self-doubt and contempt.

When I returned to work, I was reminded of how far I still had to go.

Norman Smiley, the nicest, most patient human on the earth, who played a role in hiring my underachieving ass, approached me in an attempt to push me: "You should be much better than you are. None of the other girls have traveled to Japan or wrestled in the same areas you have."

I didn't need to be reminded that I was falling short of everyone's expectations, and hearing it from someone I respected as much as Norman hurt. I knew he had excellent intentions, but I lacked motivation. It was confidence. I couldn't get out of my own way because I was so afraid of losing control of this situation.

I got through that talk without crying, which was perhaps my biggest accomplishment yet.

I even tried to argue that it was a test, as Joe had mentioned, but it was just honest criticism from an honest man. I should've done better.

But everything was changing in the wrestling industry. WWE had just launched its own network, one of Vince McMahon's brilliant financial decisions, and was leading the way in streaming apps. NXT's television show became a major selling element. Furthermore, NXT was establishing itself as the cool, edgy wrestling brand.

WWE has always flourished when compared to a significant competition. It was WCW in the late 1990s, and it is now AEW, but back then, NXT served as WWE's own alternative to Raw and SmackDown.

HHH was in charge, and he had transformed NXT into what ECW once was in the mid-1990s. Not because of the gore and hardcore mindset, but because it was a subculture of the wrestling business with wrestlers that did not necessarily fit into the usual clean mold of the main roster. The brand's purpose was to highlight the positive aspects while concealing the negative ones.

NXT was the underground, where the craft and art of wrestling were more important than biceps and triceps. While the main roster was dominated by giants, with the majority of its marquee names standing over six feet and weighing close to 250 pounds, in NXT, it didn't matter if you were five-foot-six and 140 pounds; if you could get in the ring, you could still be a huge star, and the fans responded accordingly.

What made it even more unique was that it didn't matter whether you were a woman. Women were given the opportunity to share stories and participate in the same kind of matches as males. On the main roster, the divas, as they were known, were given three minutes for each battle. If a match ran beyond time or was cut short, the ladies would be the first to go. Not in NXT, however.

Women's equal treatment was groundbreaking. And I wanted to be a part of it. This is what I came for. This was what I felt obliged to accomplish. This was my unfinished business.

Despite the fact that we were instructed at the Performance Center that ladies don't do this or can't do that, this was most likely due to an old-school notion of how the audience wanted to see their women. Hunter was unique. He did not enforce any of these antiquated rules, and he allowed women to wrestle like the competitors we were. Or, more precisely, the other girls were competitors. I was still a long way off from being on television.

But I recognized an opportunity. One of the male wrestlers developed a new character named Adam Rose. He was a rock-star type with an entourage of wacky-looking groupies dressed in absurd costumes that he dubbed Rosebuds.

And I still didn't make the cut for the human bouquet!

With no shame, I returned to Bill DeMott.

"Please, just let me be involved in some way; I promise, I'll be a great Rosebud!"

If I had to plead to be an extra, then so be it. They weren't promoting me as the company's future, and I had no reason to believe they would or should. But what I lacked in talent, I made up for with zeal.

My plea was approved.

I was going to crush this extra role. I was going to parade on TV in a brilliant blue tutu with a light-up wig on my head, acting like a total psychopath as if my life depended on it. In a strange way, it did.

I am determined to treat every opportunity as if it were my big break. When you have so little time, you have to make the most of it. I even considered becoming a lead Rosebud. Perhaps making it into a storyline in which they put me on TV and I actually wrestle!

As I stood backstage, anxiously anticipating the tomfoolery I was about to unleash on the world, I got perplexed as I listened to my fellow Rosebuds complain about not being taken seriously as wrestlers or performers. Most had never wrestled before signing with WWE and felt entitled to a push, whereas I had to grovel for this much.

I was not taking anything for granted. Fortunately, it paid off. I had done my job with such enthusiasm that when Adam Rose was promoted to the main roster, I was chosen as one of the Rosebuds to go on tour and instruct future extras how it was done!

Five of us misfit Rosebuds hopped into a minivan and traveled eight hours to Greenville, South Carolina, for an episode of Raw. It was significant enough to be shown on television but not important enough to be flown.

I was making headway with my nagging bulimic tendencies, eating a more balanced diet, and binging less, which meant my fine dresses were growing tighter and shorter, just in time to make a good impression in front of the bigwigs on the main roster. Because I assumed that was all I was being judged on (which may or may not have been the case).

With my high heels that I couldn't walk in and my dress that was so tight that one wrong move could mean I mooned the entire Catering staff, I felt so weird and unlike myself as I stood around uncomfortably introducing myself to everyone, this time with dry hands.

To my surprise, someone approached me and started a chat.

And not just anyone: he was Seth Rollins (real name Colby Lopez), one of WWE's biggest stars and one-third of the company's hottest faction, The Shield, also known as the Backstreet Boys of wrestling, alongside Roman Reigns and Dean Ambrose.

Colby held a dish of food in one hand and a sheet of paper in the other.

"Hey, I'm Colby."

"Nice to meet you, I'm Rebecca."

"What is your story?" "Why are you here?" he inquired, genuinely interested.

An avalanche of words came out of my mouth, and I told my entire life narrative up until that point, despite my very short dress and poorly done hair. By the time I finished, his dish of food had vanished.

He seemed comfortable. A familiar sense, as if we'd been friends for years. As if I could tell him anything and he'd understand.

He was a megastar and treated himself as such, yet he was also approachable and down to earth.

We talked for forty-five minutes until he was called to work.

"Good talk," he replied quietly and coolly, walking away.

"You too!" I yelled after him, nearly collapsing in my high heels, not at all calm. Or cool.

I like it up here. I'd just made a new friend.

With all of this chatting and networking, the time to work sneaked up on me. I put on my blue tutu and funny wig and made my way to the gorilla (the position behind the curtain before going in front of a crowd, named after Gorilla Monsoon, the renowned backstage interviewer) with the rest of the Rosebuds. No one was going to pay any attention to me, but it didn't stop me from feeling scared because this was my chance to shine!

It was my first time in a crowd of that size.

Stepping through the curtain, I became intoxicated with the most powerful, joyful narcotic. It was stimulating, energizing, and addictive, and I craved more. I couldn't understand how anyone would want to do anything else.

CHAPTER 14

THE DEBUT

All of that positive wrestling energy was working in my favor, because as soon as we arrived at Full Sail, the location of the NXT TV tapings, Sara greeted me with a huge smile.

"You're going to make your debut on NXT tonight!"

I looked behind to ensure she was speaking to me and not one of my traveling companions.

"Huh?! Really? Me? Amazing!"

"Yeah, it's you and Summer Rae for one section. Five minutes. You're over. What do you anticipate your finisher will be?"

"Let me think," I said, stunned.

Holy shit. Holy shit. This is it. But. I didn't have a finishing move. I had never won a bout since joining NXT. I didn't have a single character.

As the enthusiasm gave way to nervousness, I began to wonder whether this was a shit-or-get-off-the-pot scenario. But, if we're using turd references here, in this particular match, with this particular debut, I went out there and smeared a dump all over the ring and in front of the fans.

Remember when I said I wouldn't perform a foolish Irish jig on television? I lied. I lied directly to your face.

I'd been playing practice matches on the computer and, in joke, doing a ridiculous Irish jig, which thrilled the other trainers with its foolishness and my absolutely shameless embarrassment. They even sang a little song to accompany it: "Diddley diddley diddley dee diddle dee diddle dee dee," repeat.

Of course, this would be my schtick! Who doesn't enjoy an extremely enthusiastic Irish dancing clown clothed in gleaming emerald-green spandex?

It turns out I really have no shame. As bad as that was, the audience didn't care. And my God, that was dreadful. It was possibly the most terrible debut in wrestling history, with all due respect to The Shockmaster's WCW debut in 1993. If mine wasn't the most humiliating debut ever, it was certainly one of the top three. Nevertheless, the audience seemed to enjoy this foolish idiot.

When we were finished and the awfulness was over, I was overjoyed, oblivious to the dishonor I had brought upon myself, my family, my country, the firm, and humanity in general.

I have finished it! I had seen wrestling on television. I made it!

Fellow trainees crowded Gorilla, greeting me with embraces and congratulations notes as if I were Shawn Michaels, who had just wrestled The Undertaker at WrestleMania 26.

Miraculously, it felt as if I had earned the respect of my fellow wrestlers, albeit not via my jigging or wrestling abilities at the time, but rather through the effort I put in and, possibly, my attitude.

As I was exiting the building, high on life and energy, I ran into our big boss, HHH.

Perfect opportunity to speak with him and learn how fantastic he felt I was.

"What did you think?!" I inquired excitedly.

He looked at me compassionately, though I'm sure he was scratching his head, thinking, "What the fuck are you and how did you get on my TV show?" I could see you were excited. Excitement crack is what I call it. You were nervous. That's okay; everything is fresh to you. You just need to slow down, and if you think you're going too slow, slow down even more."

"Okay, yes. Yeah! "Thank you, sir." I responded, barely taking in the words and ready to run shuttle sprints in the parking lot.

That night, I couldn't sleep because I was so happy. Too proud of myself for getting there and surviving.

Welp, I thought, I guess I can say goodbye to my ambition of main eventing WrestleMania. Nobody could recover from such a low place. But perhaps I can still earn a living wrestling. Perhaps they could keep me on to promote ladies with more potential.

Over several weeks, I collaborated with Ryan Katz and Dusty Rhodes to find a more fitting character—one who had a chance of not being fired.

Finally, we deviated into generic babyface territory, substituting Irish jigs with equally enthusiastic headbanging. My new strategy was to simply scream at the top of my lungs at random intervals or anytime I felt the discomfort of a quiet crowd, combined with other anxious twitches. It wasn't good. Not good. And I rapidly took on the position of jobber, or the guy who takes the fall; in other words, the loser.

Despite my obvious inadequacies, the audience liked me, applauded for me, and wished me success. They were my saving grace.

That, and NXT had a supply-and-demand problem. Given the scarcity of female wrestlers suitable for television, I had the advantage of being adaptable and replaceable. Certainly no one was concerned with how I should be booked or protected, nor should they have been.

Nonetheless, this "jobber" role was relatively brief because they required more heels, and I was teamed with Sasha Banks, who was crushing it as her newfound "The Boss" character. And, well, every boss requires a lackey. So, lackey me up, honey britches!

I was about to turn on my friend and cherished babyface, Bayley. No one was more empathetic to the audience than charming superfan Bayley. Bayley wasn't your normal cookie-cutter gal, either. She was a true megafan who portrayed her persona to match the overwhelming love she had for wrestling. The crowd identified with her because they were her. They loathed me for betraying her.

Sure, I was consigned to the "other guy" role, but I didn't mind. I was getting TV time and the opportunity to improve at something I enjoyed.

Sasha and I were incompatible. She was all sparkle and diamonds. I was all grungy and plaid. But somehow it worked. We gave ourselves the pretentious name Team BAE—Best At Everything. We were quickly racking up wins and milestones.

NXT is now a two-hour live show, but we used to record four episodes in one night. Fortunately, they were only one-hour shows, but it meant many appearances, several battles every night, and complete chaos. However, unlike the main roster, where shows might change on the day of and even moments before, NXT storylines have to be planned out weeks in advance. This lengthier lead time provided us with an excellent opportunity to build a character, create a clear plot arc, and familiarize ourselves with the audience.

I was learning and growing quickly, establishing self-reliance along the way. I couldn't believe my luck, that every twist and turn had led me here. I was finally allowed to pursue my interest among like-minded women. Even the fact that wrestling paid for my food, transportation, and roof felt like a dream.

CHAPTER 15

WOMEN'S WRESTLING

By the end of 2014, the world had caught on. Women in NXT were booked better than the main roster, and they were finally treated equally. They had character development, substantial storylines, and well-thought-out bouts.

Emma and Paige lit the flame in NXT, competing for the first women's championship. Then, after Paige was promoted to the main roster, Natalya came down and challenged Charlotte Flair for the championship in a barn burner, with Charlotte eventually winning. The contest reminded the world of Nattie's skill, and when given more than two minutes on TV, she could put on a show to remember.

Then it was Sasha and Charlotte who raised the stakes again. Each huge match was like putting another brick to what would eventually become a mansion.

Finally, it was time for me to lay my own brick on the foundation as I prepared for the toughest test of my life. We were about to have a fatal four-way title match between what had become the mainstays of the NXT women's division: Bayley, Sasha, Charlotte, and me.

Despite my poor start in NXT, I was turning things around and making a name for myself, competing against the three best opponents I could wish for.

We were the four women who told intriguing stories, made good matches, and engaged the audience.

But more than anyone else, this was my chance. The other girls had had their turn in the spotlight and proven themselves. This was my chance to demonstrate to the world, the company, and myself that I could stand up and compete with the best of them.

I stood backstage in the brilliantly lit, cramped gray hallway, pacing and going over the match, the most terrified I'd ever been.

I have never had a pre-match ritual. I simply pace like a motherfucker, remind myself to take deep breaths, and if I'm feeling spry, I'll count to 10 to relax my ass.

Come on, Becky. Get it together. If you can't do this in front of 400 people, how do you expect to wrestle at WrestleMania? I told myself.

This was huge. But it wasn't Mania-sized. All I had to do was not stink up the joint, and I could move on to discover what true nerves were all about.

You belong here. Everything in your life has led you to this point, I soothed myself, or attempted to convince myself, I'm not sure which.

My music became a smash. I strutted out. I had moved from generic babyface to generic heel. Snarky, cocky, and mouthy. I stood in the ring, not knowing what to do with myself. Do I move? Do I stand still? What is natural? Perhaps I will touch these ropes? No, you seem awkward! Stop looking so weird, fool! I reflected as I attempted to find out how to exist in that moment while millions watched from home.

When the bell rang, I settled in. I was happy with myself because I didn't botch anything or damage the contest.

I had finally joined the conversation as one of the women who could change the game.

The wrestling community was buzzing about the Four Horsewomen, as they became known, who would permanently alter the landscape of women's wrestling. It felt like wrestling's equivalent of the Spice

Girls, with each one being unique, which was what made it so fantastic. We may all appeal to a specific demographic.

Each of us contributed something unique to the table.

Charlotte, her legacy, her athleticism.

Bayley, her passion, her technicality.

Sasha, her star presence, her finesse.

Becky, that Rocky Balboa–like heart.

CHAPTER 16

PEACOCKING

Now that NXT was touring the country as the "third brand" behind Raw and SmackDown, Sasha and I had our match outside of Florida.

We had arrived in Pittsburgh and were eating lunch at the hotel before the show when one of the referees ran over to us.

"Did you hear?" he asked.

"Hear what?" I asked.

"Dusty died."

The structure seems to have lost its air supply. Everyone fell silent, unsure how to react or digest it. We had no clue that he was not doing well. He had been walking around the school as usual, in his boots and blue jeans, educating the students and delivering jokes. Perhaps he had shed a few pounds, but in the wrestling world, everyone's weight varies.

He was the Performance Center's essence, and without him, the magic would be diminished.

His last words to me were "Shut up, Becky" as I followed him about, pestering him about various ideas I had. To be honest, I couldn't have asked for nicer final remarks.

He was the person who believed in me. The one who recognized something in me before anyone else did, including myself.

Even his last tweet was: "Lynch, @NXT Star Time she be great, top 5 of the last 5 years! Max #1."

I still didn't believe in myself, but I hoped that one day I'd be able to prove him correct.

That night, we all agreed to put on a spectacle that Dusty would have been proud of. We dried our faces, drew back our shoulders, and gave the Pittsburgh residents their money's worth.

Sasha and I went out and did our thing, pounding the hell out of each other in a championship match, which she eventually won. However, as I started walking up the ramp after the match, my leg stiffened and I began to hobble. It was that damn hip flexor again—the one that had bothered me at the start of my NXT trip.

Sasha and Bayley grabbed me a wheelchair and snuggled me into bed like if I were their baby.

It was going to be at least six weeks before I could return to the ring. And here I was, having finally gained momentum.

Sitting at home with nothing but my thoughts, I became increasingly concerned that I had lost my spot.

However, there was an outcry from the online public regarding how the women were treated on Raw and SmackDown. They witnessed what we could accomplish in NXT when given storylines and time. While on the main roster, Nikki Bella and Paige, two enormous female stars, had a thirty-second match.

The audience made their voices clear by starting the hashtag #GiveDivasAChance. It trended for three days in a row, forcing executives and decision-makers to consider giving "divas" a chance.

With all of my newfound spare time, I sent pitches for the Four Horsewomen to be promoted to the main roster. However, it appeared that the creative staff was preparing something for us. Rumors of invasion angles circulated on the computer and the internet, but it never appeared to be all four of us; it was either three out of four or two out of four. I was convinced that now since I was hurt, my name would not be mentioned, and the other three had been there longer and were considered better prospects than me.

To keep my mind off the guessing and wondering, I decided to go on a boat trip to a local lake in Orlando with a friend.

As we embarked on our maritime excursion on this beautiful day, I was surprised to learn that Orlando was more than just strip malls and theme parks, as our guide told us about the area's rich past.

Most impressively, he explained as we passed by a stunning property that the previous owner had purchased 300 peacocks to protect his home and wife while he was away! He might have acquired a guard dog, an Alsatian, a wolf, or a tiger, but he chose three hundred peacocks. Genius. I leaned over to my pal and muttered, "That's what I'm going to buy with my main roster money! Peacocks!"I

Not a minute after I said those words, a "203" number appeared on my phone, which is the area code for Connecticut, WWE's home base. When I received a call from an unknown 203 number, I knew something was up.

I answered the phone with an uneasy "Hello?"

My companion, seeing the dubious expression on my face, asked, "What's going on?" as I motioned for them to wait a damn second.

The phone rang, and a familiar voice answered.

"Hi, Rebecca. This is Mark Carrano from Talent Relations. I'm phoning because I need you on the road this weekend. I am not saying you are making your debut. They're still unsure about the creative, but they'd like you to be in Atlanta on Monday."

As I hung up the phone, I was smiling like a lunatic.

CHAPTER 17

THIS IS AWESOME

As Charlotte and I waited for our flight, grinning with anticipation, we noticed Sasha, who remained to herself. I assumed she felt, correctly, that she should make her debut on her own. She was already a star, and she deserved her own spotlight.

Our premiere happened on Monday, July 13, 2015, little over two years after I arrived at the Performance Center. Charlotte and I mentally prepared to be chastised by the established members of the female locker room. We were prepared for anything after hearing terrible stories about the hatred that new call-ups would face, such as having their clothes damaged, baggage tossed into the halls or shower, being bullied out of the makeup chairs, and other general sabotage.

To our surprise, we were greeted warmly and hugged. Everyone looked delighted to see us and kept asking, "What are you guys doing tonight?"—to which we had no response.

Keep in mind that this is a live television show. A live television broadcast that airs in millions of homes around the world. We were supposed to go live on TV in front of millions of people, most likely performing wrestling techniques, but as the hours passed, we remained entirely unaware. Even the persons participating in the secret were unaware of the magnitude of the situation.

At one point, one of the makeup artists dragged me into her chair.

"It's okay! I'm not even sure I'm accomplishing anything!" I responded, not wanting to go ahead of any of the more experienced women and unsure whether I was actually accomplishing anything. However, she insisted that if I waited any longer, it would be too late.

After the doors had opened and the live event in front of millions of people had begun, we were informed that we would be making our debut tonight.

Stephanie McMahon devised the plan to divide us into teams. Stephanie, Vince's daughter and WWE's chief brand officer, portrayed a powerful lady on television, but she was much more remarkable behind the scenes. She's a grounded, down-to-earth lady who can do it all: entrepreneur, on-air icon, mother of three daughters, ambassador, wife, and writer. She's clever, charming, and, despite being one of the world's busiest people, takes the time to talk to everyone at all levels of the ladder as if they were the only person in the world, with eye contact that is both soothing and terrifying at times. Being introduced by the most authoritative lady in WWE was the ultimate endorsement.

But storywise, we were fighting for... honor? Turf, perhaps? We didn't like the other teams because, well, we were the best. Or whatever. I'm still not sure about that one.

I was on one squad with Charlotte and Paige.

The others were Tamina Snuka, Sasha, and Naomi.

The third were Nikki, Brie Bella, and Alicia Fox.

We practiced the piece in an empty hallway in the back, so no one could see the mastery that was about to unfold in a matter of minutes.

They wanted the Three Horsewomen to look strong in the conclusion, so we focused each of our bids on a member of Team Bella.

Everything was a mess.

I wasn't even sure whether I should wear my chilly trench coat and goggles. Was I allowed to? Is now the time? Will it be awkward and clunky? What would I do with it if we started fighting? It would have been great to practice how this might play out.

I was standing in gorilla waiting for my name to be called without my entrance gear when someone inquired where it was.

I had no idea what I was doing. I was trying not to make a mistake and ended up making a lot of them. Rebecca's style is classic.

I watched intently as Paige, now in the ring, argued with the heel tag team, The Bella Twins. Stephanie joined her in admonishing the Bella Twins' heel squad for being overly prissy or whatnot. Stephanie declared that there would be a revolution once the arguing had reached its peak.

Are you talking about a revolution? Yes, ma'am. A goddamn women's revolution would be aired! However, this revolution differed from the French Revolution. This revolution involved gal-pal teams, and Stephanie was about to make significant news....

Meanwhile, in the back, I attempted to remain cool. Holy crap, this was it. I was making my debut as a character named meeeee. Not an extra; a featured player. I was a featured player. I didn't even have my damned cool trench coat.

Stephanie had chosen a teammate for Paige and proclaimed "the Lasskicker Beeeeecccckkkkkyyyyyy Lyyyyynnnnnnch."

I ran out of gorilla, and the audience erupted as if they knew who the hell I was. The gigantic black-and-yellow NXT logo dominated the 'Tron behind me.

Were they excited to see me?

To quote HHH on my NXT debut, I devised a "excitement crack" entrance and rushed to the ring as fast as my trembling legs would allow. Then he stood there, attempting to appear calm, cool, and collected. God, I was so uncool.

Stephanie continued her friendship mission. Charlotte would also join our revolutionary friend team. She was considerably calmer than I was. She walked down the ramp like a royal queen, as if she had been bred for it from birth, which she had been.

Okay, good. This was my new gang of buddies, whom I had become friends with for unclear reasons.

Which brings us to the other group of pals! Naomi came out, and Tamina expressed her desire to join the movement as well. But, happily for them, Stephanie had also recruited a companion for them! Sasha Banks is the current NXT women's champion!

I wasn't sure what that meant, but the crowd apparently did, because as the teams got into a brawl, the fans chanted "This is awesome" and "NXT, NXT!" in delight.

It was as excellent as you could expect for a debut when you didn't have your extremely cool trench coat to make you seem cool. (I'm still a little annoyed about it).

We returned to a standing ovation in Gorilla. Charlotte and Sasha were crying, and I was startled by what had just transpired.

Strangely, I felt a lot more at ease up here than I ever did in NXT. Perhaps it was the thought that I had survived, or that my employment had grown slightly more secure.

I doubt nobody in that room, or even in the arena, would have imagined that I would one day become the first woman to win the WrestleMania main event.

But they might have if I had my trench coat. Okay, I'll let that go.

CHAPTER 18

THE TRIPLE THREAT

"Shoot for the moon." Even if you miss, you'll end up among the stars.

I landed among two stars. Charlotte and Sasha were definitely the best and brightest prospects in the women's division. I just happened to be at the right place at the right moment, and I had the guts, heart, and determination to make it work.

Furthermore, I viewed my life and work as a Rocky film, because comebacks are impossible without downswings. There is no heroic defiance of the odds. And if there is one thing I enjoy, it is beating the odds.

As it turned out, the conversation with Vince worked (or management was leaning that way anyhow). They thought that it would be the ideal match for WrestleMania.

I wasn't going to get my hopes up until I reached Dallas. Not until I was in front of 110,000 fans, which is the population of Cork, Ireland's second-largest city! Even then, I imagined one of those massive circus hooks wrapping around my neck and yanking me back through the curtain the moment I went onstage.

I had previously wrestled at my favorite PPV, the Royal Rumble. I was ready to wrestle at the biggest WrestleMania yet, and another ambition was about to be checked off the list.

Mark Carrano assembled the women's roster in a room for a major announcement from HHH and Stephanie. We were surrounded by television people, and a pedestal was set up to the left with a mystery item wrapped in a black cloth. The roster waited breathlessly to see what was about to be revealed, until Hunter withdrew the fabric with a single flick of his wrist, revealing the most gorgeous thing I had ever seen. A new women's championship belt. A magnificent collection of white leather and diamonds that sparkle against a red backplate.

We would no longer be fighting for a little butterfly belt, but a full, legitimate-looking women's championship belt. They were altering the ladies' title from the terrible-sounding "divas championship" to the considerably more progressive "women's championship."

I detested the label "diva." The definition of a "diva" is "a self-important person who is temperamental and difficult to please"—a connotation I would prefer to avoid. It has been my goal since I signed to shift the term back to "women's." And we were doing it on the biggest stage of all.

I felt horrible for anyone who didn't battle for this beautiful piece of technology. Every woman on that roster helped us get to this point. However, only three of us would be involved in creating history.

Charlotte and I arrived in Dallas and got into Ric's service car. This was routine for him, but for us, it was the most exciting week of our life and the most significant match of our careers thus far.

The excitement of the city mirrored ours. Fans congregated outside our hotel, hoping to catch a sight of us. Anything that included leaving your hotel required cautious planning due to the additional time required for signature signing and picture snapping.

But if someone asked me for something, I couldn't refuse. It was the fans who had helped and carried me to this point. Waves of thankfulness accompanied me wherever I went. I found myself in tears in Whole Foods' soup aisle, reflecting on how far I'd come. Even the fact that I could now afford Whole Foods! My former idols were now friends and mentors, and I had the opportunity to make history with two women I admired and respected. It was monumental. Thank goodness no one spotted me as I wiped the snot off my cheeks and sobbed over the kelp chips in my basket.

I came into WrestleMania looking like a traffic cone, with freshly dyed orange hair, an orange-tinted spray tan, and a bright orange jumpsuit to match.

We had already put the bones of the match together, but it lacked oomph and bravado. We still didn't know who would win and were pulled in a million different directions.

This was a historical WrestleMania for women. It was rare for the women's title to be defended at WrestleMania, and there were two women's matches on the card! Only a few years ago, the women were standing in gorilla, ready for their battle, when it was cut short due to time constraints. We'd gone a long way and were laying the groundwork for decades to come.

I sat in the stands, looking out at the massive stadium, thinking how it would look in a few hours as my opponents performed their ramp arrivals. Charlotte was being taken to the ring by her legendary father, and Snoop Dogg, Sasha's cousin, was going to serenade her there. I was at the intersection of pop culture crossovers. Becky from the block, who presumably required no practice but numerous punches in the arm, because what the hell was going on?

After the stars had finished rehearsal, we convened in a practice ring in the back to work out the wrinkles of the bout, attempting not to be distracted by the deaths of megastars such as The Rock, "Stone Cold" Steve Austin, and Hulk Hogan. This match served as a springboard for future inclusion in the same category.

After much deliberation, it was determined that Charlotte would win by tapping me out in the center of the ring. I knew my prospects of winning were small, but the opportunity to dominate my friend at

WrestleMania was the next best thing.

Besides, I didn't have to win. In vengeance for Rumble, I planned to make a suicide dive, or torpedo through the top and middle ropes onto Ric Flair at ringside, and it was as significant a victory as any.

There was nothing left to do but do it.

I stood behind the curtain in gorilla, sensing the excitement of the 110,000 enthusiastic spectators in attendance. (Yes, there is discussion regarding this number, but shut up.)

The fans were eager to see the beginning of a new era. We had the chance to set the table, transform the way women were portrayed in the industry, and steal the whole show.

And as all of this spun about my thoughts, I felt a sense of serenity wash over my entire body. I was ready. I was prepared. I was surprisingly relaxed. How can this be? I was nervous before every match I'd ever had. And yet, here I was, in the biggest match of my career, and I was as calm as a cucumber.

My music played, and I walked out, head down—as was my habit at the time. Sure, Becky. Let's freaking go. You are extremely cool! I reflected on my tranquil mood, feeling like an incredible rock star.

Only when I looked up and saw all the supporters crowding the massive stadium did I pee a little. Not symbolically; I actually peed a little (ha-ha). I hypothesize that I was so terrified that my body refused to tell me because it feared I would die. Lest I roll up into a gorilla and cease to exist. Thank you, body; you're a real friend.

I stood in the ring, taking in the immensity of the place, as the others made their dramatic entrances. I occasionally looked down to see whether there was any exposed urine on my shorts.

My head couldn't quite grasp what was going on as we went through the battle, narrating, "Yeah, fuck yeah, we are killing this shit!" However, I am unable to hear how the audience is reacting.

Are they in awe of our greatness?

Sheamus had warned me weeks before: "It takes a while for sound to reach you in these large arenas. You may have made a motion just a minute ago, and you can hear them react even if you appear to be doing nothing. Sometimes the sound simply leaves and you cannot hear anything." I felt as if I couldn't hear anything as we went through our collection of maneuvers and sequences. Charlotte crashed on my head from a suplex at one point, and I could feel my eyelid getting cut, expecting for the blood to spill and interrupt the match, ruining this history-making moment. But it never arrived. I was wearing so much mascara that it acted like a clog, saving my ass as we went on—I dove on Ric, Charlotte moonsaulted from the top turnbuckle to the outside, there were frog splashes and dropkicks, and my goodness, we were cooking. All of this culminated in Charlotte delivering her signature finisher on me and Ric preventing Sasha from making the save on the floor. Charlotte thanked me, and I tapped out, "We did it, woman."

I took the side ramp back to the gorilla, shedding adrenaline with each step as the audience slapped my hand in delight.

Sasha followed closely behind, collapsing in tears as we reached the back. Lita was there to embrace me: "You did it, kid; that was fucking great."

Great, now I'm weeping. Everyone at Gorilla gave us a standing ovation. Follow that, fuckers—all three of us shared the same collective thinking. We'd made history.

CHAPTER 19

LET'S GET READY TO RUMBLE

While WWE may not have thought I was the one yet, the guy I was seeing clearly did. When I returned to Los Angeles, he organized an evening out with me, taking me to the arcade at Santa Monica Pier.

"Let's go on the Ferris wheel!" he said.

"I'm not really feeling it today," I said, without mentioning that I'm a terrified little baby when it comes to heights.

Oh, come on! "It'll be fun!" he encouraged, dragging me toward the rickety coaster.

I climbed in slowly, afraid, holding the sides with a death grip. When we reached the top, the Ferris wheel came to a standstill.

"Oh no! "It's broken!" I cried, dreading Rebecca Quin's death.

Just then, he stood up and began shaking our capsule, which terrified me even more as he dropped to one knee and withdrew a small black box.

Oh no, I thought, how could we have such radically divergent perspectives on this relationship?

"Will you marry me?" he said, opening the box to reveal a pear-shaped diamond ring. Or, as I see it, a teardrop.

"Yes," I replied, like a fucking coward. What should one do? If you're not ready to end the relationship right away, it's best to say yes and then break up when it's more convenient for you.

As we hugged and I pondered how the heck I was going to get out of this, the Ferris wheel began to move again.

As we stepped off, a photographer and a man popped a bottle of champagne and a huge arrangement of flowers.

At least I had said yes; otherwise, this would have been completely embarrassing.

I kept the ring from public view, embarrassed to wear it. I would question my happily married friends repeatedly, "How did you know they were the one?"

"I just knew," they'd all say, sounding like clichés.

That cannot be true. Surely you go through the same agonizing doubt every day of your life, wondering how you're going to get out of this. Surely?

It's entirely understandable not to want to notify anyone about your engagement, especially your mother. It's not uncommon to hide rings in images, or to believe for a moment that you'll never actually do it.

The few friends I told about my situation were all quite nice. Recognizing that I would eventually reach my own conclusions, they gave me the customary "as long as you're happy" spiel.

Colby was not one of these friends, and when he found out, he instantly contacted me, "What the fuck are you doing? You were in my room a few months back, crying about this motherfucker."

Jeez, guy. Don't yell at me, I reasoned.

"Yes, I understand. Look, I'll be honest. I do not think I will go through with it. But how are you expected to respond if you're not ready to end the relationship?

"Fair, fair."

At least he understood. Unlike my mother, who refused to speak to me for three weeks when I finally told her.

"I'm not going to marry him," I insisted.

"You are ruining your life. You just told me at Christmas he's not right for you!" she scolded.

It was the worst when she was correct.

The weight of the guilt was terrible, making it difficult to maintain the "I'm a star" atmosphere that Shawn Michaels mentioned.

But I'd need to get my act together fast. The dynamics of the women's division were set to shift due to two factors.

For the first time in history, the eponymous PPV would include a thirty-woman Royal Rumble. The winner would advance to a championship contest at WrestleMania.

It was already monumental for me to compete in my favorite PPV, The Royal Rumble, let alone in an actual Royal Rumble. In addition, I was one of the first two people in the match, alongside Sasha Banks.

I knew I had no chance of winning—that was reserved for Asuka this year—but what actually got the world talking led me to:

Number two, WWE has signed MMA phenom and former UFC champion Ronda Rousey. Ronda, the catalyst for change in women's MMA and the reason women were allowed to compete in the UFC, had transcended the sport to become one of the most well-known figures in popular culture, appearing on magazine covers, TV shows, and in films. And she became one of us.

After Asuka won, the champions of each brand (now Charlotte for SmackDown and Alexa for Raw) entered the ring to give her a choice. Ronda Rousey was ushered through the group of sweaty wrestlers as her signature entrance music, "Bad Reputation" by Joan Jett, blasted in the arena, much to the delight of everyone in attendance. She stormed down to the ring, pointing at the WrestleMania sign.

But what did this mean? Was she going to have a title shot? Did she really know how to wrestle?

The entire world was buzzing with the same questions.

The historic signing of one of the world's most famous athletes to WWE overshadowed the Royal Rumble.

But how did the women who had been working tirelessly for years feel about this?

Personally, I felt both excited and nervous. It was a fantastic testament to how far we had gone that someone of Ronda Rousey's quality wanted to be a part of our division.

If we had still been restricted to thirty-second matches and bikini contests, I doubt it would have been an appealing idea for her. Rousey's signing with WWE had the ability to throw a light on women's wrestling like never before, which I was thrilled about for all of us who had worked so hard to be viewed as equal stars to males. But I was anxious because I hadn't received much attention during the last year. With the arrival of this global star, I wasn't sure whether I'd ever be featured again.

We would be on different brands, but I hoped that one day we might meet in the ring if she decided to stick with it.

Despite the title of her entrance music and the things I had heard about her attitude, she was beautiful. She was thrilled to be there, smiling and welcoming us all to the massive entourage that surrounded her.

She wasn't used to the "competition" being so kind and supportive. But this isn't true, since it takes two to make money. And Ronda was a moneymaker. She would not make her in-ring debut until WrestleMania, which is two months from now.

The build for WrestleMania was underway, and I was not involved in any of the big match negotiations. Or any match, really. While Asuka elected to confront Charlotte for her championship, I was demoted to the battle royal on the first show. That is where all wrestlers who are not assigned matches are transferred. It mostly acts as a reward for the wrestlers who work their butts off every year, ensuring that they will still have a slot on the card and a respectable salary, even if it is a token gesture and a match that no one cares about.

I expressed my disappointment to Sami.

"I feel like I work so hard, but I can't seem to break through."

"You know, man, just enjoy it. Every year, WrestleMania feels like so much pressure. But I participated in the battle royale last year, and it allows you to fully immerse yourself and take in the surroundings. Try to accomplish that."

"That's a great way to look at it," I admitted. And he was correct.

I took his advice to heart. But, my God, all I wanted to do was be the main event of that show. It is the ultimate aim of any wrestler, and it has never been accomplished by a female. But I couldn't even get on television; how could I expect to be the main event?

I was trying to follow Sami's advice, but after hanging out with Charlotte and hearing her talk about her match and their ideas, I'd be lying if I said I wasn't jealous. I felt terrible about this. I should've been happy for her. I should've been inspired. That if it could happen for her, it might happen for me someday. But, darn it, after years of being a bridesmaid, I wanted to be the bride. But not the bride, because her home life was terrible.

When Mania arrived and I went out for the preshow fight royal, Sami was correct: I could have taken it all in more. I got to look around the stadium and see how excited everyone was to be there and experience it.

There is nothing quite like performing in front of such a large crowd. And when you let yourself take it all in, you don't want it to end.

However, I was thrown out so abruptly and with so little emphasis that most people had no idea I was no longer in the running.

I went to the back and cleaned up before watching the rest of the show.

Ronda's match was fantastic. She was in there with the best leaders she could have asked for, HHH, Kurt Angle, and Stephanie McMahon, who had gone over every detail painstakingly.

Charlotte and Asuka also hosted a barn burner.

My friend texted me, "How great were Ronda and Charlotte's performances this year? It must be them in the big event next year!"

My instinct told me I was going to be the main event.

I got ousted from the preshow with no one giving a shit. I had no reason to believe I could ever be the main event, but there was a teeny tiny voice telling me I could, and I was moderately upset that this friend hadn't noticed it.

But in the meantime, I drowned my sorrows in large amounts of complimentary champagne at the after-party, irritating Colby with my inebriation and wailing about my tear-shaped engagement ring, which I now dubbed my "ring of sadness."

CHAPTER 20

MONEY IN THE BANK

I awoke unexpectedly one night, about 3:00 a.m., lying close to my fiancé, when a small voice in my head stated, "All your dreams are on the other side of this relationship." I wanted to thrive in my business and main event WrestleMania, but in my personal life, I aspired to marry and have children. Just not with him at my side.

After four months of engagement, it seemed inevitable that this would come to an end.

For several weeks, I told myself that the next time we fought, it would end. So I'm not proud to admit that when that disagreement did occur, when I was out of town and over a text message, I ended it.

He moved out while I was in Europe for a two-week tour. I felt horrible; I liked him, but I knew it wouldn't work. I recognized it from the first time we met: I simply craved the company in this often isolating industry. And that was extremely inappropriate and selfish of me.

My work life began to bloom after I had freed my personal life of the hole I had dug for myself.

I felt like a magnet for positive energy. I felt free, alive, and completely invincible.

Suddenly, I was more involved at work, invested in my friendships, and more creative.

We were approaching the Money in the Bank PPV. And I would take part in this year's ladder match. Maybe, just maybe, I thought, they would give me the briefcase.

I'd worked so hard, and people still admired me, largely because of my underdog position and internet presence. When I wasn't on TV, I would go to WWE's digital crew and film everything. An interview and a ridiculous pun video. Or I can create my own (discovered) hilarious videos or stories for social media. But it would at least allow the internet audience to get to know me when I wasn't being featured on television.

Charlotte was also going to be out of the picture following this match since she needed surgery, so who better to win?

Alexa Bliss! That is who.

Oh well, there's always next year, I reminded myself.

"Who should be the last person on the ladder before Alexa wins?" our producer TJ questioned the group.

"I think Becky would get the most sympathy," Nattie added.

We were the first match on the main event that night, and the Chicago crowd was as boisterous as always.

I went behind the curtain not knowing exactly what to expect. We assumed it was a nice match, but was it? We assumed they would sympathize with me the most, but would they?

I took the ring first, while the other girls scattered to hunt for ladders. The audience immediately began screaming my name. Oh, that's good, they like me!

Whether it was a semi-Irish connection between the locals and myself, or if they actually believed I'd finally pull one out, they rallied behind me like I was their hometown gal. As soon as I put my foot on the bottom rung of the ladder, the applause and cheers became audible.

I eventually reached the top of the ladder. The briefcase was in my hands. But where is Alexa? Fuck. She was late. I was fumbling, trying not to take the briefcase and win by accident while yet not appearing to be a complete moron. Finally, what seemed like 10 minutes later, she arrived to alert me to a chorus of booing.

I fell against a ladder below and bounced out of the ring. I watched Alexa ascend to the top and unhook the case. A mix of shouts and whistles echoed around the arena.

Well, I thought as I massaged the goose egg on my head, I believe everything went well.

We all dragged our broken bodies back to Gorilla, where we were greeted with a standing ovation.

"It was the right call to have you up there last," TJ said. "I think they liked you," he added, grinning like a Cheshire cat.

The next day, the crowd's positive reaction to me became the buzz of the town. It's not often that someone catches fire with little momentum, so when it did, podcasters and internet outlets alike urged WWE executives to take note.

Which they did—and propelled me to become the top challenger for the SmackDown women's championship against Carmella at SummerSlam that year.

After two years of failing to win any gold, I was finally getting a one-on-one title bout at a huge pay-per-view event. It seemed like me and the audience were on a tandem surfboard, riding the WWE wave together.

Could I be the confident, unapologetic champion that I wanted to be in 2016? Only time will tell.

Or will it?! Oh no! This is Wrestling! We need conflict, debate, and betrayal! Kind of.

Charlotte, who had been away for surgery, returned quickly after her absence. You could cut an arm off of that woman, and it would regrow a week later. Nothing kept her down, and almost nothing kept her out.

In an act of valor, she dashed out to save me from a brutal thrashing at the hands of the evil champ.

Charlotte offered me a hand up after she had completed her mission of chasing Carmella away.

I'd rather have accepted the pounding with honor than be spared a whopping while displaying weakness. I wanted to be able to stand on my own two feet, whether I succeeded or failed.

Her interference earned her a spot in our bout. The crowd was furious because the championship would now be contested by three people.

Charlotte had been so extensively featured when we were called up three years ago, and the audience thought that this was my moment to shine, and she had squandered it.

Ultimately, this was Creative's plan. Charlotte was going to win SummerSlam, and I was going to flip a heel on her. And the creative team couldn't figure out how I would be the babyface in this scenario.

Not only would Charlotte win the triple threat—on the night that, in the fans' views, was supposed to be a big coming-out celebration for me and my return to the top—but she would pin me to do it while I had Carmella on the edge of taping.

A message from the production office stated that the turn needed to be justified. Justified? But was I the bad guy? They were about to transform me into a fierce mega babyface.

When the day arrived for SummerSlam 2018, I questioned one of the writers, "Are we really doing this?"

"Yes, the understanding is that you'll likely get a babyface reaction here in Brooklyn, but that's just 'cause they're a heel crowd."

If done correctly, this was going to launch my career like never before. After years of taking a backseat, I was not going to let this opportunity pass me by.

That night, before heading out, I was warned about a few things.

"Because this is a heel crowd, they'll likely cheer you when you turn."

It's not because they're a heel crowd, but that's fine.

"Don't look at them in recognition."

"No problemo."

At the end, I had Carmella in my finisher, and as her hand raised to touch the mat in submission, the crowd was on their feet cheering, "Bam!" Charlotte attacked me from behind with her finisher "natural selection."

One, two, three.

"Annnnnnndddddd neeeeeeewwwwwww." SmackDown Women's Champion Charlotte Flair."

While I sat there looking heartbroken, I heard a combination of shouts and boos. Internally, I was as delighted as could be, knowing that this would be the pinnacle of my career.

Charlotte stood above me, title in hand, sorry face, as the tension in the building grew. She benefited from my anguish, and everyone knew it. I stood up and approached her, the crowd afraid of what was about to happen. When I hugged her, they let out a chorus of boos. They despised the fact that I refused to speak up for myself, that I would simply accept passing the baton again.

Charlotte held me and murmured, "This is your moment. Give it all you have."

So, I did. I smacked her so hard that the PE instructor who had failed me all the way back in Ireland and time could feel it. The crowd let out its loudest pop of the night.

As I maintained my gaze on her, attempting to summon venom and anger in my eyes, I couldn't help but think, "This is foooooooking cool!"

The audience was yelling "Becky" and "You deserve it," which could be construed in two ways: either it was aimed at her and she deserved to be beaten. Or they realized this was the beginning of a new trip for me. A new push, and I earned it.

I did as I was told and never looked up at the audience. Though I desperately wanted to take them in. We had gone on such a journey together.

I headed back towards the gorilla, only looking back at the damage once more before passing through the curtain.

Charlotte quickly followed me through, and we hugged and thanked each other.

"Are you okay?" I inquired.

"Oh, yeah, woman, I'm good," she said unconvincingly and standoffish.

I knew she was upset. I'm not sure whether she was injured physically or mentally.

"Are you sure? I smacked you quite hard."

"I'm fine, seriously," she insisted, tears welling in her eyes.

Watching her on television might lead you to believe she is untouchable, yet she is an emotional and sensitive lady who wants to be appreciated.

In the story, she was supposed to be the nice guy. But everyone could relate to my story. The person who always tried their hardest. Was never the best, the strongest, or the most naturally endowed, but possessed heart, fire, and determination. They understood what it was like to be passed over for a promotion or not invited to a dance. Charlotte's narrative was far less common. Most people are not born famous, multi-champions, or with goddess-like physiques. The storyline was completely wrong. I knew it, as did she. But it worked in my favor.

CHAPTER 21

I AM THE MAN

I was scheduled to face Charlotte for the SmackDown women's championship at the Hell in a Cell PPV.

The audience was already immersed in this domestic feud between two former best friends, and I pushed it as far as I could to make it feel authentic, wanting each match to have that "big-fight feel" about it. I was pounding every platform with purpose. And the goal was to get people to care. Promos, social media, interviews, everything matched because I was "living the gimmick," which meant portraying the character outside of our TV shows. I frequently pushed the boundaries, seeing how much I could get away with and frequently following bad advice, particularly when it came to social media and mean-spirited tweets. Many of the things I said at the time make me regret them now.

I understand that controversy generates revenue, but it also breeds bitterness and self-loathing. Proceed with caution when sending out harsh tweets.

Charlotte and I set together our title battle fairly haphazardly. The underlying and relatively unspoken tension between us was like a pink elephant in the room.

I knew I was going to win, so it didn't matter how we got there. Even though this was a new character and I'd have to change my style to fit in, I wasn't concerned with looking strong or outdoing her. In fact, I always believe it is advantageous to strive to make your opponent appear as good and strong as possible. That way, if you win, you've surmounted a hurdle; if you lose, you've got a hill to climb. Taking Colby's counsel from a year before, I explored various ways to "get my shit in."

On this night, September 16, 2018, more than two years after earning my first and only title in WWE, I would win my second. Only now was I in a far better situation than before.

I won by quickly catching Charlotte and countering her spear with a pin. One, two, and three.

Creative advised that she try to shake my hand afterward, but I, as cocky as ever, refused and mocked her by shoving the title in her face. That'll have the crowd booing! they reasoned.

It didn't. If anything, it made them happier. They enjoyed how I didn't care about anyone's approval. In reality, I hope I could be like this. I believe many others did as well. That is why it worked.

This tale was planned to run until the end of October, ending in a last woman standing bout at the first-ever all-women's PPV, Evolution, which will take place on Long Island. Charlotte and I will be working together on three PPVs: Hell in a Cell, Super ShowDown in Australia, and the Evolution blowoff match. There was enough story to keep the audience interested without overwhelming them. And maybe, just maybe, we can get over all of this and be friends again.

We already had excellent chemistry, and it improved with each match. As friends, we strike each other hard; as foes, we beat the crap out of each other. And when I say Charlotte is strong, I mean freakishly powerful. In Melbourne, Australia, in front of 50,000 people, she struck me so hard that she severed a nerve on the left side of my mouth, which took nearly five years to heal. Actually, I was just looking in the mirror. I am not convinced it has totally healed.

I hoped the massive swollen lump protruding from my lower lip went unseen until Daniel Bryan, in the middle of a post-show talk, blurted out, "Was that always there?" while bending down and squinting to get a close look at my slightly distorted face.

"No, I had hoped no one would notice. "I was hit in the mouth."

"Yes, I see that. And, no, it is really visible."

"Thanks, Bryan."

Fuck.

Good thing my character didn't care about her appearance or what others thought of her. Rebecca Quin did, however, and it took me a long time to see myself speak again.

With all the momentum I'd been building since SummerSlam, the firm was doing everything it could to profit on it. They were even bringing back wrestling legends for me to collaborate with. They organized a promotion for me to face Edge, who had been open about his support for me throughout my career. His career had ended prematurely several years earlier due to a neck injury, thus seeing him back in a WWE ring was a highly anticipated event. And for me, as a fan who has adored him since I was an angst-ridden teen, it "reeked of awesomeness."

Edge, as beloved as he was, was entrusted with convincing the audience to boo me. Surely, if I faced a legend like him, people would decide to despise me. "What do you think about this?" he asked as he sat alongside me at a table in Catering, offering suggestions for how the promotion should proceed. I'd never worked side by side with someone of his stature and expertise before, and while I was eager to do whatever he asked, his treating me as an equal and as if my thoughts mattered made me feel like I had arrived.

"What if I warn you about the path you're taking, and tell you that you won't like yourself at the end of it all?" he said enthusiastically. "What would you say back to me?"

I was frightened to speak out and react. He was a Hall of Famer. A excellent in the industry. I didn't want to be out here pitching bad ideas to a legend.

"Maybe I lean into it?" Like I don't like myself, but I love myself?" I asked.

"Yeah! That's fantastic!" he said, giving me the courage to continue.

"Then, would it be too much if I said, 'Get out of my ring; don't hurt your neck stepping through those ropes'?" I inquired, hoping not to offend anyone who had returned to work with me particularly. Despite the fact that I had been insulting my former closest friend for months in our storyline.

"Not at all!" That is perfect!" Edge replied.

When the words came out of my now-deformed mouth live on TV, despite the clear disrespect to someone the audience adored, they cheered me. We had a special bond, which was amazing. For me. Not Edge's neck.

"I tried!" Edge yelled to everyone in Gorilla as he stepped back through the curtain.

"They're not going to boo her!" He shrugged and laughed it off.

To add to one legend's appearance, I was at a hockey game with Mick Foley the same weekend. It wasn't lost on me that the same girl who had failed PE was now hanging out with all of the heroes she had admired on television.

What a freaking life.

At the game, I received a text message from a friend that read, "You should call yourself 'The Man.'"

The concept was simple yet divisive. In our sector, like in many others, there was a long history of bright people at the top of their game referred to as "The Man," but they were all men. Now, the "brilliant" person was myself.

"What would you think if I started calling myself The Man?" I asked Mick for a second opinion.

"It's genius," he said with a grin.

I shared a photo of myself brandishing my championship in Edge's face, captioned "I am The Man."

We now had a slogan for the movement. It was powerful. Anyone can be The Man. It didn't matter what your background, gender, or occupation was. You simply needed to declare your greatness and not let anyone convince you otherwise.

CHAPTER 22

POINT TO THE SIGN

The Rumble came before WrestleMania's big event. I was ready for my first match with Asuka, the current SmackDown women's champion and one of the greatest wrestlers of all time.

She is a delight to deal with. Between terrible English and charming giggles, she brings a variety of ideas, as well as the most incredible footwork and grace I've ever seen. When she passes through the curtain, she transforms from the kindest human on the planet into an utter killer, and it was an honor to face her for the championship, and even more so to put her up for it. I planned to lose to her in the first match of the night before competing in the Rumble later that night.

I needed the match with Asuka to go well. If it didn't, they might not want to see me again that night. Or, as the obnoxious voice in my head said, they won't want to see me ever again.

When I arrived in Arizona, the location of the Royal Rumble that year, Colby graciously offered to pick me up from the airport. He had arrived earlier that day and hired an Airbnb to stay. "You're welcome to join," he said. I declined. I had to concentrate on my matches, darn it, and I didn't need any man with a god-given body to distract me.

I may have touched up my makeup and spritzed myself with perfume before getting into the car.

The drive from the airport to the hotel was only 10 minutes, but we talked in Colby's car for about two hours. I despised how simple it was and occasionally wondered what it would be like if we kissed. Derailing my own thoughts by reasoning that his beard would most likely leave a rash on my face, which would be quite uncomfortable.

Indeed.

It was getting late, and I had an early start the following day. We held for a few more moments than it should have before I went back to my room and texted my friend Jay, "I think I may be in love with Colby."

To which he replied, "I just turned on my phone and it appears to be broken." What? You literally just gave me a laundry list of all the reasons why this would be a horrible decision this morning."

"What can I say?" Becky, who is single, is unpredictable.

It's a poor idea, I would tell myself.

But you are single, Becky. You are free to pursue whatever interests you. No attachments. You get anything you want out of it. You're a strong, independent woman!

Oh, absolutely. I wasn't experiencing feelings. I was launching a goddamn movement. Thank you very much, Gloria Steinem. I was a regular.

The next day, the night before Rumble, Colby invited me to dinner, but I didn't finish my appearances until midnight. So he tried to convince me to visit his Airbnb with a selfie.

We're playing the selfie game, right? To be honest, I wasn't really into selfies. I frequently mocked the youngsters for their insatiable desire to send selfies. Are we quite conceited? Is this arrogance? Look at me; I'm so gorgeous that you'll fall passionately in love with me after seeing my lovely but only slightly manipulated photo of me pouting like a duck, which is how I believe the selfie sender's inner monologue goes. What happened to seducing someone with wit? What about intelligent quips? A joke, perhaps? I'm not exactly sure. But this was how the youth were doing it these days, so I decided to fit in. And "kids" refers to Colby, a fully grown adult male. I was not sending any selfies to children.

Anyway, my middle had a glimpse of abs on this day, assuming I flexed correctly in the ideal lighting, and I thought I'd share them with someone. Even if I was thinking, "I really shouldn't," that is usually how the finest things begin.

He answered with heart emoji eyes, and we kept messaging like ecstatic teens.

I hardly slept that night. Selfie excitement, anxiety, and anticipation of what was to come all took its toll on sleep.

The date was January 27, 2019. The Rumble where The Man appeared.

It took place at Chase Field, a big baseball stadium that could hold up to 40,000 people. I stepped out to a shout from the audience. Fans clutching "The Man" placards illuminated the arena, and I was overwhelmed with appreciation. My favorite pay-per-view of the year, and this time I would win the Rumble at the conclusion of the night. Thirteen-year-old me wouldn't have believed it. Thirty-one-year-old me barely managed.

In the end, it was down to me and Charlotte. However, not before a salty Nia, who had just been eliminated, knocked me down the stairs and hurt my knee. I'd have to overcome as many challenges as possible on my route to the top.

The officials were about to call the contest, crowning Charlotte the winner, when I bravely hobbled into the ring and, after a series of strikes, tossed her over the top and performed the one thing that every wrestling fan turned wrestler dreams of doing: the classic point to the WrestleMania sign. Once you've done it often, the referee will yell at you, "Keep pointing!" I'll tell you: it's a tremendous shoulder pump.

I returned through the curtain to a flood of congratulatory hugs and back pats. As I did my rounds, I noticed Charlotte was crying. I didn't ask why; we weren't that close anymore. I figured she was over her WrestleMania moment. But I knew she'd be included and that she'd always be OK. Not because she is Ric Flair's daughter. But she was good. And she had a work ethic that never failed her.

However, the night was not yet over. I still had to watch Colby win the Rumble.

It was so fortunate that these two flirtatious friends were having the best Rumble evenings of their life. In this true love story, one character abandons monogamy while the other remains doubtful of the other's intentions.

Anywhooooo. Colby had been suffering back difficulties; he had fractured his spine in a match a few months earlier but hadn't told anyone since he's a machine who can fight through anything and didn't want to pass up this opportunity. He was also contending for the WrestleMania main event berth. I watched uncomfortably, knowing he was about to go through a table in the middle of a match, and praying to the heavens that he didn't make a big mistake. That would have certainly dampened all of the flirting.

When he came through Gorilla, there were camera crews waiting to capture him. I hugged him as I clumsily tried to get out of the shot. This flirting had gotten quite blatant, and I didn't want to give the game away on camera.

I was working out in the hotel gym when Colby announced that he was on his way. Flustered, I finished my set and dashed upstairs to shower before meeting him in the elevator. My body language conveyed my nervousness as I desperately tried to fight it. You are The Man, remember. You are the freakin' Man. Goddamn, why can't you just be The Man in real life? I argued with myself.

What the hell are you so worried about? This is your pal. You know it isn't going anywhere. Just have fun and stop being too serious.

"Mind if I get changed?" he inquired as we entered my room.

Why do you need to be changed? I thought, but I said, "Make yourself at home," my voice breaking like a prepubescent kid.

He didn't go into the bathroom or try to be modest; instead, he stripped down to his underpants in front of me, quads sparkling as sunshine cascaded into the room.

Fuck. It's going to happen, Rebecca. There's no point in fighting it now. Claim dominance! I thought.

"Would you like a kombucha?" I asked for the most millennial pickup line ever.

The minifridge in my room was right beside the bed, where he was seated.

"Sure. "What do you have?"

"Mint mojito, strawberry serenade, raspberry hibiscus…"

"I'll try the raspberry hibiscus."

I bent down to collect the bottle, then straightened up and handed it to him. The kombucha, that is.

This is the time. You've got this, Quin. You are the man!!!!!

I stepped right over him, straddling his legs as he sat on the bed.

He'd spoken a fine game. It's time to see if he can back it up.

He seemed nervous.

I knew I was right because of how he said, "I'm nervous."

Our lips touched, and we were soon in full make-out mode.

So this is what it felt like to kiss him, beard tickling and tongues rolling. My heart is beating. Years of sexual tension and energy culminated in this single instant.

"I wasn't expecting that," he stated later.

Bitch, of course you were. You had been building the groundwork for several months. I wondered if it had been years. But I said, "Me neither."

We both lied.

"We should go," I replied, finally halting its progression. We had the entire night ahead of us.

Raw had an early call time, and I felt like the new kid in school. I was a SmackDown resident, and being in this new environment put me on edge.

Colby and I didn't see each other all day, but we texted and flirted, remembering those romantic hotel moments earlier that day.

But, back to the task at hand. This was the moment everyone had been waiting for. I planned to face Ronda Rousey at WrestleMania.

Coming off the highs of the previous night and events earlier in the day, I was feeling fairly good about myself.

Unfortunately for Ronda, she had just had a promo where the crowd chanted for me, which diverted her stream of thought, followed by a poor match. However, it made my arrival a little more exciting. And we needed all of the enthusiasm we could garner to secure that main event place on Mania. But given my emotional butterflies, what was at risk, and days of no sleep, I was nervous to say the least. I managed to present a promo that appeared to be calm, cool, and collected, which was followed by Ronda's riled-up promo in retribution. This time, she was enraged by the crowd's shameless bias, as well as by me.

As a result, I began doing double duty on Raw and SmackDown, a situation that would last until WrestleMania. TV time is valuable real estate for a performer, but as a babyface, if you get too much exposure, the audience may tire of you.

Which is exactly the risk I was taking by pushing things with Colby. We work together; what if we grow tired of each other?!

Nonetheless, I waited for Colby to finish in the hallway of the Phoenix arena, trying not to make it obvious that we were going together.

We returned to my room, closed the door, and immediately began pawing at each other. Clothes were tossed across the room, and I kept thinking, "Ahhhhhhhhhhhhhhhhhhhhhh!" My friend Colby is going to see me naked. What if he's not into it, and everything becomes awkward from here? Abort the mission! Abort the mission, Rebeccaaaaaaahhhhhhh! Oh, but it feels so good and he looks great. Beck, you're in too deep now. Well done, failure.

But on the outside, I attempted to appear confident and stumbled my way through. This new degree of intimacy has the potential to fundamentally alter our relationship.

Lying beside him felt so good, but I couldn't get over the fact that I was in bed with a lifelong friend and had just experienced him in a whole new way.

I was thinking less about, "He's the one," and more about, "I wonder how we'll get out of this without feeling weird together."

CHAPTER 23

THE INTERGENDER TAG

"Seth tells Corbin to pick whichever ref he wants. So he chooses Lacey because she has a vendetta against you and tries to cheat Seth out of the title; that's when you show up. What do you think?" Ed Koskey, Raw's head writer, presented an idea to me.

"Oh, I don't know. Is it unusual for The Man to have a man, you know?" I wondered.

"Think about it," Ed replied.

Colby and I hadn't even been dating for six months. Our relationship had just been public for a month. Collaboration may be enjoyable, but will it be effective?

"The way I see it, it's like seeing Daredevil and Elektra fighting side by side: if you know they're together, that's cool, but if not, it's no big deal," contended Colby.

"I suppose as a fan, I'd want to see that," I replied.

"Exactly, and it'll be fun," Colby repeated.

"I'm worried that they're just going to turn me into your girlfriend, like that's what I'll be relegated to," I confessed.

"Nah, you're too big for that by now," Colby assured me.

The summer months following Mania and before SummerSlam can be a bit of a downtime in WWE. Think of it this way: Christmas brings out the mania. There's so much buildup, anticipation, and preparation, and then the big day arrives, you get all of your presents, and you're left in the frigid dreariness of January, where nothing significant happens.

Joining forces with Colby would either excite or destroy us. From both a job and an interpersonal one.

After considerable discussion, and with the earth-shattering ecstatic love energy between us, we gave the creative team the green light to proceed with the storyline.

But I had one condition that needed to be pounded into Vince's mind.

"Becky can't just be Seth's girlfriend."

"Ha-ha! Becky is not Seth's girlfriend! Seth is Becky's lover, ha-ha-hah-ah-hah-hah." Vince exclaimed, laughing hysterically.

It was all really great in theory. Two of WWE's top talents, both champions, square off against evil.

We made our side-by-side debut at the Money in the Bank PPV and quickly discovered that it was a complete mess and not at all cool.

Every two minutes, commentaries reminded viewers that "Becky and Seth are in a real-life relationship"—which was both uncomfortable and off-putting.

We also had no notion how to engage with each other on screen. I was accustomed to being a badass. He was, too, and in this gooey, confused TV relationship, we were simply awkward. Or, more accurately, I was simply awkward. Or "cringe," as the term was frequently used to characterize it online.

Blending the two worlds did not work for me since I was two different persons in each of them.

In the ring, I stated what I meant, didn't take shit from anyone, needed no one, and exhibited no vulnerability or humility.

At home, or with Colby, I didn't need a mask. He was well aware of the insecure, odd, and frequently quiet girl I was, who struggled to express her feelings or speak up. He knew all of my weaknesses, for better or worse. He understood I wasn't the person on screen unless I was angry. Then The Man would be afraid of Rebecca Quin.

I believe everyone was relieved when the storyline concluded. Him. Me. The audience.

Colby and I learnt a lot about ourselves and each other in that short amount of time. We hadn't been dating very long, yet we were pushed into the deep end.

Even if we weren't a good match onscreen, I'd discovered the right person for me offscreen.

We went on our first vacation to Hawaii two months after the TV storyline finished at the Extreme Rules PPV—and after we had our first tag bout together, which, despite the terrible storyline, was actually a tremendous match.

On our second day on Maui, we got lost returning from a day trip and discovered a gorgeous hidden beach. Nobody was there, just the sun setting behind the cliffs, the sound of the water slamming against the shore, and the occasional bird tweeting in song. I was photographing Colby as he gazed at the sunset, his jacked back and sleek tattoo more attractive than the magnificent scenery. He suddenly whirled and went to his knees.

I stopped snapping when my jaw touched the sand below.

"Will you marry me?" he inquired.

"What? Is this real?

"Yes," he answered.

"Yes! Yes!" "Of course!" I exclaimed, "I am happier than ever."

A lady with a professional camera appeared seemingly out of nowhere a minute later. Colby had not planned any of this, but when we discovered the ideal scenario, he thought it was great. And the magic lady took my iPhone and positioned us for optimal lighting.

As we regained our bearings and returned to the hotel, I texted everyone I knew to let them know the wonderful news.

There was no shame, worry, or hesitation.

As a buddy, I never expected Colby to marry, but after two months of dating, he was already calling me his wife. We never actually considered marriage; it was more of a given that we would be together forever.

My mother did not stop talking to me for three weeks after I told her. She was quite happy.

When you know, you truly know.

CHAPTER 24

GIMME A HELL YEAH

Things were moving at breakneck speed. Over the course of a year, every wrestling dream I had ever had came true. I was featured on the cover of the WWE video game for the first time ever as a woman.

I appeared on magazine covers, including ESPN The Magazine, where I was the first wrestler to do so. I did SportsCenter advertisements.

I spent a week straight sleeping exclusively on flights since I had appearances all over the world.

I got to work with The Rock, John Cena, Edge, and film with "Stone Cold" Steve Austin.

I appeared on Billions on Showtime.

I did some filming with Marvel.

I landed a book deal. (Hi!)

I became the longest-tenured Raw women's champion in history.

I purchased my first house.

I had some terrific matches. I had terrible matches. I had several underappreciated bouts. I had several mediocre matches.

I was able to travel the world and work alongside my best friend and now fiancé while being compensated.

Life was a sequence of ups and downs, with little time to analyze or be conscious of what was going on.

However, I suddenly had several voices in my head and ear, each offering different advice. Some voices were more influential than others, and some ideas were superior to others. It was my job to maneuver through the chaos; after all, I was The Man. But I occasionally fought the wrong creative battles and listened to the wrong people. I got agitated about insignificant promotions or outcomes. Approaching everything as if it were life or death. I felt compelled to comply with what I had been doing on social media, namely, being an asshole, which made me feel bad about myself. I felt like I hadn't been true to myself, and to take a passage from the opening of the book that my father had constantly repeated to me (which he misquoted from the Bible, but I preferred his version): "If you bring forth what is within you, what you bring forth will complete you. If you do not express what is within you, it will destroy you."

I adored my work. I despised how wound up I would become over every single week of television or creative direction. As if the wrong story would return me to the pit of irrelevance from which I had come.

I'd fought so hard to be the first woman to headline WrestleMania and change the course of the industry, but after I got to the top, the first question was, "What next?"

The corporation came and gave me a quite large contract, but now that I had accomplished my ultimate goal, I wondered if it was time to consider my next goal. One outside of the ropes is being a mother. I had desperately desired a family one day, and I had found the perfect spouse.

At work, I was feeling increasingly concerned about my booking. Having reached the top of the mountain did not mean I could enjoy everything more; rather, it meant I was preoccupied with staying there. And I'm confident I was a pain in the ass for the creative staff.

It's so clichéd to say that the journey is more important than the goal, but it's true. The destination was simply the start of a new trip. But, as I was terrified about what would happen next, the world abruptly shut down.

Colby and I used less caution than normal after Raw, as we were in the grips of intoxicated love. Even though I wanted to be a mother, I was still the champion, and I fully expected it to take an eternity to become pregnant, despite the fact that I was only thirty-three, given the damage I had caused to my body over the course of over two decades. Between pimples and eating problems, I believed my insides couldn't possibly be working properly.

Oh my, was I mistaken.

When we got home from filming WrestleMania on the PC two weeks later, I was already feeling nauseated.

No, it couldn't have happened that rapidly.

Holy shit. But what if it did?

There will be no fans for months. What will I miss? If there was ever a moment to be pregnant, it is now.

But what if I lose my momentum? Everything I've worked for could come crashing down.

This had never been done before. How will Vince respond? How will fans react? How will my mother react? Out of wedlock, and all that jazz.

There is only one way to find out.

Take the darn test, Rebecca.

I purchased one of those early reaction tests; "6 days earlier," it stated.

I urinated on the stick. The control line appeared first, but not the second, the "You're pregnant" line.

I threw it out without waiting the full time since I was quite positive I was not pregnant.

I went to the gym, feeling as nauseated as a sailor.

When I returned, I saw the stick again, but this time there was a second line.

"Oh, shit."

"Don't read after 10 minutes," the box stated.

But that's the second line. I swear it's the second line.

I showed Colby.

"Oh, shit. That's the second line!"

"Right?! But it warns, 'Do not read after ten minutes.'"

"When did you do this?"

"Before the gym."

"Did you not read the instructions?"

"You know I'm not an instruction reader."

"Oh, fuck. Do another one."

So, I did.

Another weak line.

"I think that's positive."

"It's very faint."

I texted Rachel the next day to show her.

"It looks negative," she remarked. "Do not be disappointed. It typically takes a long time.

But I feel it! "I feel like shit."

"It might just be your period. My sister tried for a full year."

I'm getting a digital test!

Life hack: always take the digital test.

I visited the drugstore to pick up the test. As I walked out with the box in hand, the man behind the counter said, "Good luck."

After I finished reading the instructions, Colby and I camped out in the bathroom, waiting for the little digital window to tell us our fate. Those three minutes felt like we were waiting for the full length of Schindler's List.

"Pregnant," Colby announced as he threw his arms up in the air! Proud of his seed. "Yaaaaaaaaaaaaaas!"

Holy stuff! Yes! But also, no! What if I'm not really ready?

I AM NOT READY!!!

Now all of those questions were valid. "What will Vince say?" I inquired, while maintaining that I should not have to care. I was a woman and had the right to become a mother. Sure, it wasn't ideal that I was the current champion. Men in our industry do not have to forego the essential part of the choice of starting a family, so why should I? Apart from the obvious reasons for the time away. But this is a new world, and these things must be taken into account. For better or worse, I was going to be a crash test dummy. Could women wrestlers have it all?

Colby texted his mother a photo of me holding the test. She called right away and began opening up her wardrobe, displaying all of the baby clothing she had already purchased in preparation for this day.

"Damn, Holly. "We haven't been together that long."

"I thought I had more time; that's why these are the only things I have," she explained, pulling out a full baby clothing.

Oh, man. I'm about to become someone's mother.

We completed the rounds.

We phoned Colby's father.

We called my mother.

We called my father.

The fathers cried.

Our lives were about to change forever.

CHAPTER 25

I AM THE MOM

The week before my due date, I became quite terrified. I am not ready.

Everyone would ask me, "How do you feel? Are you excited?"

I'd say, "Oh my god, I can't wait," but inwardly I was quivering with anxiety.

What if I didn't form a bond with her? What if I developed postpartum depression? As it stands, I tend to lean toward depression.

On a rare day off from the gym, Colby and I sat in his coffee shop and relaxed while watching two young girls play on the couches.

"We're going to have one of those."

"I know!" I replied with a hint of anxiety.

A moment later, the phone rang.

"Hi, is this Rebecca?"

"It is."

"Hi, this is Dr. Jones."

"Hi, Doc, what's up?"

"We examined your liver enzymes, and they are now elevated. You have cholestasis. So we'll bring you in to induce you."

I grabbed Colby's arm as he was saying, "Who is that?" What's happening? I certainly had a horrified expression on my face.

The doctor explained, "Because if it crosses past the placenta, it will stop the baby's heart. Given that you're 39 weeks pregnant, it's preferable to get her out right away."

I promptly said, "Oh, shit. Okay, we'll go right there," before telling Colby, "We need to have the baby right now. "They're going to induce me."

Panicked, he exclaimed, "No!" What?! No! What's going on? No!"

"We need to! Actually, Doc, could you please explain this to my husband? (We hadn't married yet, but "fiancé" is such a flowery word.)

A minute later, he hung up the phone. "We are going to have a baby!" Ahhhhh."

I assume I wasn't the only one who felt nervous. Though I was visibly shaking. The realization that life will never be the same again had occurred.

We rushed home to get our hospital bags. People had advised me to eat as much as possible before going to the hospital because I would be unable to eat once there.

I stood at the kitchen counter, shoving leftover pad Thai into my mouth, my entire body quaking in panic, my hunger nonexistent, forcing the food down despite the fact that swallowing felt like throwing up in reverse.

The next time we returned home, we'd bring our little girl along.

I had been in labor for 24 hours without pain medication and was now puking and spasming violently due to the discomfort. The most painful part of the experience, in my opinion, was the obnoxious high-pitched nurse informing me, "Each contraction brings you closer to meeting your baby."

Shut up, bitch! I'm vomiting over here. What if I don't like this baby! It sounds cold and callous, but I'm 98 percent certain that many women have felt the same way on the verge of giving birth. Transitioning from someone's child to someone's parent in one fell swoop.

I had promised myself that if I could get through this without an epidural, I would be able to do whatever else I wanted in life. I would have the willpower, determination, and fortitude to do anything. For I am the source of life, the fortress of agony, and the willer of wills. Or something like that. The point is, I hadn't had a challenge in a long time, and I was becoming rather bored at home.

The Pitocin rushed through my veins, never letting the agony subside for a second. As Colby dived into his snack, the loud crunch of chips and the strong smell of salsa added to the experience temporarily. As I snarled, "Go away," a serpent's tongue briefly emerged from my mouth.

"What's that, honey?" he said affectionately.

"Go away, please."

"Huh?" He sounded bewildered.

My head felt too heavy to look up.

"These chips. Go away. Please go away."

He sighed and placed the crinkling bag away. "I'm so hungry."

I had crossed the threshold. Shit was going on.

You know, movies offer a very terrible impression of labor. I thought the pushing was the difficult part. But as soon as I felt the desire, it felt like a relief, like if my body was finally working with me rather than against me.

Sure, the guttural sounds I made were similar to those heard on Animal Planet. But it was not painful.

After pushing for five minutes, the doctor informed me that the baby's heart rate was decreasing.

"We have to get this baby out now," she told me firmly yet quietly.

I was done waiting for contractions before pushing; I bore down and pushed that child out with every ounce of my being.

However, she was not crying.

Why didn't she cry?

I had never been so afraid in my life. After nine months of wondering if I would bond with this baby, I was prepared to die for her.

As they slapped her on the back, the nurse covered the baby's mouth with a handkerchief.

"She can't breathe!" I shrieked at the nurse, removing the cloth from my baby's nose and mouth, utterly forgetting how umbilical cords work.

Thirty of the longest seconds of my life passed, I was relieved when, with one more smack to her back, she began the most lovely, amazing tiny moan I had ever heard. My darling newborn girl was here. She was the most beautiful thing I had ever seen, and I adored her with every cell in my body.

Nothing will ever be more important to me than her.

We named her Roux. I thought that was a really clever name.

However, when she sobbed, she appeared to be a grouchy old lady, more akin to Agnes than Roux. We still nicknamed her Roux.

I couldn't believe that this wonderful kid, who I had no idea how to care for, was mine to keep.

Two days later, we returned home. My lovely little family.

CHAPTER 26

AND NEW

I was on my way to Los Angeles, eight months after having Roux, when Vince McMahon called.

"What would a comeback look like at SummerSlam?"

"Damn, I don't know. You've just called me. What are you thinking?"

"Well, I suppose you showed up and cost Charlotte the title. Then go away again."

"What's the story behind it?"

"There is none, just a one-off and then we don't see you again until the draft."

I was insulted.

They had told me I'd be back for SummerSlam, but then they changed their minds and said I wouldn't be back until October. They had changed their minds again.

I had plans to make. A baby to care for.

"Can you give me a night to think about it?"

"Of course, of course."

When I got off the phone, I told Colby, "This fucking guy…," and began explaining the call.

To my surprise, he answered, "Ha-ha!" I sort sorta like it. Just the thought of you banging someone over and then disappearing. "That sounds like something Austin would do."

"What do you think?" Like, they don't have a plan. It feels like a waste of my return."

"No, guy. It is not your actual return."

I considered it from an outside standpoint. I let everything boil and went to bed, pretty excited to be back in the mix. Let us fucking go.

Only to wake up the next morning to a text from Vince saying, "I've changed my mind. But be ready."

"Well, that is disappointing. I'd come around to the notion. But don't worry, I'm always ready," I said.

I'd completed all of my in-ring training and was in the best shape of my life, but I still had more time to prepare.

Only a day later, on a Saturday, Colby, who was working live events, texted me, "Sasha's out."

She was supposed to battle Bianca for the SmackDown Women's Championship.

SummerSlam was only one week away. I was going to get a call saying they needed me.

Sunday came. No call.

Monday came. No call.

Tuesday arrived... Brrrring, brrring.

"We need you for SummerSlam."

We had talked about our friend Jen, but she was going to SummerSlam as a fan and was excited for her first large event. I had no idea what I would need for this stupid comeback. New equipment? I did not have any of that.

Thank goodness I'd dyed my hair a week earlier.

Turning heel was a big step for me. I'd spent my whole WWE career as a babyface. The one time they attempted to transform me into a heel, I became an even greater babyface. But this was different. It may work this time. Because I had been given so much before leaving to have Roux, the online crowd was already turning on me as a babyface, and screwing over someone they genuinely cared about, like Bianca, who was new and exciting, and the crowd was genuinely behind and happy for the push she was getting, would be the most heinous thing I could do. And I was eager to try out a new character, the polar opposite of "The Man."

By Friday night, I still didn't know what I was doing! Communication was limited due to both uncertainty and a desire to keep this a major secret. Thankfully, Jen, the angel that she is, stated she would miss the show to assist us, eliminating my major cause of anxiety.

Around noon on Saturday afternoon, Johnny Ace, now head of talent relations, and Bruce arrived on my and Colby's tour bus, which we had recently acquired. We couldn't travel fifty-two weeks a year, staying in a different location every night, with an infant who didn't have one.

Bruce, Johnny, and I had a formal conversation amidst the craziness of what would soon become everyday life on the bus. Important business meetings were taking place while Roux crawled around the floor, cooing and wailing, Jen picking up toys, Colby making meals, and our bus driver, Andy, pottering around, seeking for things to mend lest he remain idle for a single second.

Sasha was out, and I was in. It turned out they had a minor issue with their original notion. They had forgotten to book Zelina for the PPV. So instead of a two-on-one match, it would be only Bianca and

Carmella.

I'd then come out, beat up Carmella, and throw her out of the ring onto the steps. Cut a promo challenging Bianca to a title match that would "blow the roof off the place" and then easily defeat her.

Bruce began, "Vince just wants one thing."

"Well, I can do that!" I responded, happy that I wouldn't have to start with a full match with someone I'd never worked with before.

Johnny said, "So you go to shake her hand, punch her in the throat, and then one thing—what would that be?"

"Probably a Rock Bottom?"

"That sounds amazing. We'll inform Bianca and get her in here as soon as possible so you can discuss it with her."

"How about Carmella? Does she know?"

"No, we'll tell her in gorilla. Trying to keep this as private as possible."

Bianca came in to visit me a few hours later. The turmoil on the bus had been heightened by the addition of a hair and cosmetics artist, Megan, to the equation, with Roux continually attempting to remove brushes from Megan's hands as soon as she approached my face.

I stood up as Bianca walked in, giving me a big hug and smiling as she welcomed me back. I didn't know her well, having only met her a few times, but she could not have been more gracious.

"We'll make you a huge babyface out of this." "Thank you so much for being so cool," I told her, attempting to assuage her concerns about any potential fuckery on my part.

"I understand how it goes. I'm really delighted to be a part of this moment."

I knew she was being honest. I can also assume she is not an android and was really upset. She'd been doing an excellent job as champion.

My goal was to ensure that she had a big moment at WrestleMania.

It would have been easy for her to complain about being buried, to be nasty to me, and refuse to cooperate with me, and all of this would have been understandable. She exemplified great class and tact, and her next championship should be even bigger.

I fled from the ruckus at the front of the bus to the rear bedroom and called The Rock to make sure it was acceptable to use the Rock Bottom, as I didn't want to just steal his finishing technique. Not only is he the world's most successful movie actor, but he's also like Batman: he's always available when you need him.

"Of course," he said in his beautiful manner of saying everything he has ever said. "This is your moment. Take it in. And when the moment comes, I want you to look into the camera and just say, 'I'm back.'"

He's the freaking best.

It was almost showtime.... I fed Roux one more time before handing her over to Jen, ready to do the dang thing.

I was hurried past everyone in line, including John Cena, HHH, and Stephanie, all of whom smiled and waited at the curtain, waiting for my music to play.

All these thoughts were running through my head, including, What if they don't remember me? What if the pop isn't that big?

My fears went almost immediately when my music played and the audience cheered as if we were still friends, sending shivers down my spine.

I was too delighted and excited to remain cool. To use HHH's words from years ago, I was on "excitement crack."

I once knocked Carmella out of the ring, which didn't garner much of a pop, partly because I suppose most people thought she didn't deserve it and it was mean-spirited to the woman who had turned up to cover for another's absence.

It was game on: the audience got ecstatic, sensing the intensity of what was about to happen. This wasn't the match they were expecting, but by god, it was the one they wanted right now. I soaked up all of their joy and love for one last second, knowing that in about a minute they would loathe me. Alas, ol' pals, I thought, it's been a nice run, but I've done everything I could as your friend; now it's time for me to see what I can do as your foe.

We had a little moment of good sportsmanship with a handshake, and then bang! Right inside the kisser! Slam! Right on her back! One, two, three! "Annnnnnnnnddddddddd neeeeeeeewwwwwwwwww!! SmackDown Women's Champion, Becky Lynch!"

The air was pulled from the arena. The pop had faded into boos, or mostly astonishment and perplexity. What the hell happened? Did they just squish Bianca? Why? How?

My heel turn had started. People were actually angry.

It would be difficult for someone who had previously been a fan favorite to suddenly become the bad guy. However, if they believed that the machine was behind me, that I didn't care about anyone else and intended to preserve my seat at all costs, they would undoubtedly be angry. And they were very angry.

When I returned, I saw Bianca crying. Understandably. She felt as if her momentum had been killed; nonetheless, she would not sell it. She's a real-life champion who pretended to be thrilled for me. I attempted to convince her that I would do the right thing for her, but she didn't know me and had no reason to trust me. I'd have to prove it to her.

As I made my way through the sea of wrestlers and colleagues I hadn't seen in nearly two years, greeting me and offering hugs, I was eager to find my baby. Show her my new title—"Look what Mama did!"—as if she would give a damn. This was my new world, the ideal combination of what I loved and who I loved the most.

Instead of going out to dinner to celebrate my return, or hanging out with my friends, talking shop and cracking jokes, I microwaved a frozen meal and ate it while nursing my child; then it was time to bathe her and put her to bed. I couldn't think of a better way to celebrate. Or a better way to conduct my life from now on.

EPILOGUE

THE DARK MATCH

What came after SummerSlam in 2021 and into 2022 is my favorite year in wrestling. As a heel, I suddenly felt free to do whatever I wanted. To say whatever I wish. To avoid taking myself too seriously or having to meet anyone's expectations.

I gained a fresh perspective on life and work. I was there to develop my opponent, tell the greatest tale I could, and possibly get an entertaining ass kicking in the process.

Wrestling is my art. And I'm damn excellent at it, despite not being the world's most technically talented artist. My body is my paintbrush, the ring is my canvas, and the maneuvers are the paint. There are my opponents—different strokes for different folks—but it's all art, and what the viewer thinks is entirely up to them. But, for me, all I want is a body of work and a portfolio that I'm happy with.

Even though I was back on the road four days a week, every week of the year, my new little family accompanied me the entire time. Sure, it meant taking a tiny baby to Saudi Arabia and back twice, or to and from the UK multiple times, and flying several times a week. It meant not sleeping through the night for a single night throughout the year. Sometimes you don't sleep at all the night before a major PPV. I was overjoyed with the love I had at home. The majority of the audience either disliked me or played along. Twitter is where the true animosity occurs. Where avatars in droves informed me how bad I was. I might despise myself. With my gorgeous little baby, hot-ass hubby, and ideal job, life has been fucking great.

Of course, there were some hiccups. I fractured my trachea. My and Charlotte's heated rivalry reached a boiling point when we had one of the shittiest segments in SmackDown history, when I felt she deliberately went off script during a title exchange, resulting in me yelling in gorilla that she was a, to use my exact words, "crafty fucking cunt" right in front of Vince and a slew of onlookers, and her emphatically denying it was intentional.

And, yes, Sasha and Naomi walked out of Raw right as it went live when we were supposed to be the major event that night, causing havoc, but they had their reasons, and that is their book to tell.

Vince abruptly retired from WWE after being everything I'd ever known, and he is in many ways responsible for my current existence and my lovely little family.

I was able to have my dream match with my teenage hero and buddy Lita in Saudi Arabia, where women were previously prohibited from competing.

Bianca and I were able to make up for her short loss by stealing the freaking show, if I do say so myself, at WrestleMania 38 in Dallas, where I had my first WrestleMania match six years earlier, and I got to give her her championship back. Eventually, our conflict lasted until SummerSlam that year, when I ultimately turned back babyface but also separated my shoulder. In some ways, this was a good thing.

And my tiny kid has seen it all, indifferent to her own way of life. I get to be her constant. When everything around us is changing, from never-ending airports and hotels to sleeping on buses and in various towns every night, her mother is always there to put her to bed and comfort her when she wakes up.

I've learned a lot on my path, many of which are clichés. That it is always about the journey, not the destination. Change is always possible, and nothing is impossible until someone does it. That nothing outside of ourselves can provide enduring contentment. More than anything, I've discovered that my biggest opponent has always been self-doubt, and that when I can break free from its bothersome shackles and have the guts to follow my inner compass, wonderful things can happen.

I had never considered myself successful, since I was constantly pushing to accomplish more, be more, and chase more. That hamster cycle had grown quite tiresome until I realized I had all I had longed for as a child. My family, desired job, and friends. For a girl who was always so typical in every way—average height, average weight, average fears, average grades, and average upbringing—I've had the opportunity to achieve some quite extraordinary things.

I AM THE MAN, THE MYTH, THE CHAMPION!!!

The contents of this book may not be copied, reproduced or transmitted without the express written permission of the author or publisher. Under no circumstances will the publisher or author be responsible or liable for any damages, compensation or monetary loss arising from the information contained in this book, whether directly or indirectly. .

Disclaimer Notice:

Although the author and publisher have made every effort to ensure the accuracy and completeness of the content, they do not, however, make any representations or warranties as to the accuracy, completeness, or reliability of the content. , suitability or availability of the information, products, services or related graphics contained in the book for any purpose. Readers are solely responsible for their use of the information contained in this book

Every effort has been made to make this book possible. If any omission or error has occurred unintentionally, the author and publisher will be happy to acknowledge it in upcoming versions.

Printed in Great Britain
by Amazon

54394576R10086